I0036509

SHORTCUTS
GET YOU LOST!

A Leadership Fable on the Dangers of the Blind Leading the Blind

MARK VILLAREAL

ISBN: 978-0-692-75108-4

Copyright © 2016 by Mark Villareal

All rights reserved. No part of this publication may be reproduced, stored in a retrieval system, or transmitted in any form or by any means without the prior written permission of the author or publisher.

Effect – The power or capacity to achieve the desired result; influence.
The condition of being in full force or execution; goes into
effect tomorrow

Affect – To have an influence on; bring about change in.

Affect and effect have no sense in common.

As a verb, affect is most commonly used to mean "to influence" (how
smoking affects health).

Effect means "to bring about or execute" (layoffs designed to effect
savings).

The American Heritage Dictionary
Second College Edition
Houghton Mifflin Company, Boston, MA

DEDICATION

In loving memory of my good friend, Stacy McRee,
and my always loving and supportive parents,
Christobal and Mary Alice Villareal.

TABLE OF CONTENTS

ACKNOWLEDGEMENTS

I have had a lifetime of learning and a lifetime of growth. The day I stop learning will be the day I am ready for the grave, as truly that is what keeps my blood flowing. As I have learned to imitate those I admire and those I have learned from, I truly desire to pay it forward like my mentors have taught me. If I can make a difference to just one person, then I have made a difference. This is how I benefited, from unselfish mentors, whom I thank so much.

I must acknowledge my parents, as they laid a solid foundation, and allowed me to live through the rewards and suffer the consequences as they loved me so much that my character was more important to them than my comfort at the moment. Thanks Mom and Dad. To my brothers and sisters, being the youngest of the bunch sometimes had its advantages, and also its disadvantages, but you truly filled our household and relationship with love.

As stated, I have had so many mentors that to name them all may be impossible, and some of you may not know you were being observed. Jack, not sure where you are today but you set me in the right direction. Doug Darnell, Steve Hockett, Paul Gaines, Mark Smith, you all were there to assist in my growth, thanks. Dave Koker, Steve Akins, Ken Hagerstrom, Mike Benvenuti and our teammates, you each set examples and challenged me outside my comfort zone. To great supporting friends Marty Berg, Jeff Bottom, Chuck Weisbrich, Ivan Jackson and Tim Chestnut thanks for your belief. To my brothers in Christ Doug Robbins, Rob "Scribman" Scribner, Dwight Keys and Ben Posey, thanks for your prayers and your faith.

Mike Newman, I cannot thank you enough for all you have done. Keith Martino, you are one to watch and observe as a true example of one that lives his values. To those who assisted on this project and for your encouragement, Emily, Crystal, Kelly, Lisa, Christine, and of course Laura, your encouragement, advice and assistance meant everything. Finally, to my 5 Point Enterprises family, Derek Wright, Scott Hardin, Jamie Fiely, Scott Riggs, Don Arnett, James Cox, Bill Allen, Tiffany Wallace, Vicki Burris, and Kendra Dehm thanks for the "first Team" environment we live and share as a team.

Bob, thanks bro, you have always been there.

CHAPTER ONE

CRAP OR HONEY?

As one that studies business, I have witnessed many successes and many failures. I often question how some managers are consistently more successful than others. What do they do differently? What is it about certain leaders that allow them to be successful no matter what circumstance or situation they find themselves in? Think about an athletic coach who can take over a struggling team and immediately impact success with the same players, the same managers, and the same coaches. The only change was at the top. What is that individual's secret? Obviously motivation is a factor, but what motivation? What brings about success?

With this question and objective in mind for managers and leaders in business, I set out to find key answers. One road of the journey led me to Mr. Scott and the answer of CAUSE AND EFFECT.

Mr. Scott was a successful manager for a large corporation, a sales based organization providing a service product. This company had locations in most major cities worldwide. Researching Mr. Scott, I discovered that he had, at different times, managed several of these locations. At each location, Mr. Scott had success. Each location was different in circumstances, yet Mr. Scott still was successful. At a brand new location, Mr. Scott started from scratch. Success. The next location was a struggling one, yet with the impact of Mr. Scott, that location soon became successful. Another location, success. Utilizing the same management staff and personnel, Mr. Scott gained success quickly. His leadership not only sustained growth but also developed key qualified personnel who advanced up the ranks benefiting the corporation at headquarters and other locations. Even while experiencing these personnel losses, locations continued in their successful ways and always seemed to have the right replacement. Was this luck? Was it the demographics? Was it the economy? What did Mr. Scott do that others could emulate?

Prior to contacting Mr. Scott, I did some research of his past employees that had worked at some of these locations. In fact, it was a past employee that had first led me to Mr. Scott. I was intrigued with how highly this person spoke of his former boss with no underlying obligation to do so. After all, Mr. Scott was not his employer anymore. I then contacted other former employees. Each spoke freely and openly with admiration consistently expressed for Mr. Scott, his motivation and his management style. In my discussions I did find some who had disagreed with a decision or a policy, but it did not diminish their respect or opinion of Mr. Scott. One of the best testimonies is how others speak of a person after their experience with them. Much like death, it is how others speak about you when you are gone. I was impressed with the respect these past employees had for Mr. Scott.

I then called Mr. Scott's office, expecting to reach his voicemail as it was around the dinner hour, and was surprised when Mr. Scott himself answered the phone. Introducing myself politely and professionally, I explained I was researching business leader's success strategies. Mr. Scott's openness and warm demeanor put me at ease. I asked many questions, including his educational background, and I was a little surprised that it was nothing extraordinary. I inquired about his past work history prior to this present corporation. Interestingly, Mr. Scott had been in three totally different industries, yet still very successful in each position.

At the end of our conversation, I expressed my appreciation for his willingness to share. Mr. Scott asked if I had anything else that he could help me with. I paused, and then asked him what he believed was the one key to his success.

Mr. Scott stated, "I have been fortunate to have good people work for me."

"I am sure you have," I replied, "but your history shows that you have achieved success in each place that you have been."

Mr. Scott interjected, "I have been fortunate to have good people at each place I have been."

I admired Mr. Scott's humility, as he gave credit to others instead of seeking it for himself. I redirected my question by asking about his management philosophy.

His reply: "Allow employees to enjoy their job; support employees all you can; and never forget about cause and effect."

"Cause and effect? What do you mean by that?"

Mr. Scott answered by saying, "Why don't you come visit our business so you can see for yourself?"

"Thank you! Sure. That would be wonderful," I said. "When would be a good time and how much time can you set aside for me?"

"Young man, I will gladly give you all the time you need. I do suggest for your benefit that you spend time with my management staff and our employees."

"Sounds great," I replied. "How much advanced notice would you need?"

"Tomorrow would be fine," he said. "Our work day begins at 8am, but I'll be here at 7am. Why don't we meet then?"

I accepted his offer.

I arrived the next morning slightly before 7:00am. Being respectful, and forgetting to ask about their dress code, I wore a dress shirt, tie, and a suit coat. I figured that meeting at seven would allow us ample opportunity to speak before the arrival of other employees. I expected to encounter a quiet, empty setting, but I was greeted by the receptionist and escorted in, surprised that the office was already full of employees getting organized for the day ahead. The receptionist introduced me to Mr. Scott, who appeared younger than I perceived from our conversation. Mr. Scott was probably in his mid-forties, wearing a nice suit, and was well groomed. He politely showed me around, then we went into his office, which was in view of the employees.

As I entered Mr. Scott's office, I noted its simplicity. There was no oversized desk, fancy chair, or any other luxuries, just a simple desk and chair. On the wall, Mr. Scott had four computer-made signs. The first sign read, "A little change in DNA and you'll get a frog, when you could have had a prince." The next one said, "Follow up, support, and reaction." The third sign stated, "Rewards or consequences?" And the fourth, "Cause and effect!"

There was no way to not take note of these signs, so I mentioned them to Mr. Scott. "Obviously these messages must have meaning and significance to you for these signs to be so prominent in your office."

"Yes," he answered. "Each is its own reminder to me for different things. They are so important to me that I keep them visible to remind me throughout each and every day."

"I would like to ask you about them. Can we start our discussion here?"

"That would be perfect."

"This first sign: A little change in DNA you'll get a frog, where you could have had a prince. Can you explain?"

"Sure," Mr. Scott replied. "I am not afraid of change, in fact, I embrace it. But I caution others because too many times in business when we are not getting the results we desire or expected, we panic. We make drastic changes, when only little ones are needed. We do this out of desperation, and most of the time, without giving adequate thought. Now thought does not take long, but mistakes do. Mistakes cost time to correct. In our eagerness to succeed, we sometimes change things at a moment's notice. I could say that haste makes waste, but it goes deeper than that."

I nodded.

Mr. Scott continued, "This sign reminds me that even a little change can make the result much different. And the more time in which that change develops, the more different the result. Let me use a couple of examples. First, consider the male chromosome in a fetus that determines a male child. Take that chromosome away and you will have a female child, the complete opposite. Now a more drastic change over time would be the example of the boy growing up next door."

"The boy growing up next door? Please explain."

"Yes, imagine a boy growing up next door to you wherever you lived as a child. If you took a two-week vacation, when you returned home, the boy would still look the same to you. However, that boy did grow and mature some during that time. The changes were so subtle that they were hardly noticeable. But if you moved away for a few years and then returned, the changes would be more significant and even drastic. Yet, if you had been living next door the whole time, the changes would have seemed very subtle."

"So what does that mean?" I asked.

"It tells me that I have to be careful about the process of change. First thing to consider is what the results are that I desire. That is called starting with the end in mind. Then I need to look at the specific thing I am considering changing and ask myself if what I am changing is something that had a positive result before. If it had positive results at one time, I need to access if it needs a complete overhaul or is it just an execution problem. Many factors play into the decision to make change. This is what I call the cause and effect moment. That's why you are here, are you not, to learn about cause and effect?

"Yes, I am. Mr. Scott, can you explain what you mean by cause and effect?"

Mr. Scott paused before he replied, "Young man, let's do an exercise today. Spend the day here visiting with my management staff and employees. You are welcome to observe and ask anything. I sent an email after our conversation last night informing them of your visit. I informed them of nothing else. I am sure that you will find them open and helpful."

"Thank you, but before I visit with them, I would like to talk with you some more about the other signs on your office wall."

"Certainly."

"The next sign: Follow up, support and reaction. What is this about?"

Mr. Scott did not hesitate, he simply smiled and started in, "Follow up, support, and reaction are what I, as a manager, promise each employee. It is also what I expect from my management staff."

He continued: "Follow up means to be open to each employee's needs, wants, and ideas, and more importantly, it is up to the leaders of the organization to follow up on those wants, needs, and ideas. It is imperative to not leave an employee hanging. Nothing can be more frustrating to an employee. Follow up and you will gain trust. Fail to follow up and you will lose trust. It is that simple. This sign is my reminder to make sure I follow up on what I said I would. If it will take a little time, then I make sure to communicate that to the employee."

Mr. Scott made eye contact to make sure I was following him. I smiled and nodded for him to continue.

"It is crucial that you let your employees know that you have not forgotten about them. Follow up quickly on whatever you can. Don't let things pile up on your plate. And follow up even when it is not expected. Communicate and be honest. A false statement to buy time will lose integrity. I once witnessed a manager, we will call him Joe, who would lie to his employees on issues large and small. An employee would ask Joe if he was following up on their situation and Joe would assure them that he was. Joe also covered up the situation to his superior. Had Joe asked for help he would have received it.

"Eventually the employees realized that they were not being told the truth. This took their focus away from their job. More importantly they lost faith and trust in their manager. On future situations they were apprehensive to even approach him. Joe lost credibility with the employees. This had a profound effect on productivity. You gain trust or lose trust depending on your follow up. With proper follow up, each employee feels important, because they are important."

"That makes sense," I agreed. "What do you mean about support?"

"We strive to support our employees as much as possible. True support is actually seeking what their needs are, and not waiting on employees to voice them. How many times does your boss ask what he can do to assist you?"

I shrugged.

Mr. Scott smiled. "It is my goal to approach our employees each day with this question with the expectation from management that we'll respond. The environment created is one of open communication, which is motivating to employees."

"I would think so." I was impressed.

"When we ask an employee what he or she needs," Mr. Scott went on, "we expect an answer. It's not just a rhetorical question. We show by our follow up and support that we are genuine. The employee who does not speak up, but witnesses the follow up and support his fellow employees receive day after day learns to express his own needs in the days to come."

"I know I would! I would want a manager that is genuine in wanting to help me succeed." I liked what Mr. Scott had to say.

"Exactly. You want employees hungry for your help and assistance, not avoiding it. If our response is genuine, our effort will show. Follow up and support feed on itself, and is a true benefit to management."

"Can you explain that?"

"Absolutely," stated Mr. Scott. "The more we as managers are involved in our daily business environment, we become naturally more informed and aware. Surprises are few and far between. This creates not only a good environment for employees, but for managers also. Instead of employees being protective, they are open."

"Sounds like a great environment to work in. Now can you explain reaction?"

"Of course," Mr. Scott said. "The word reaction reminds me to be proactive and certainly we strive to be, but reaction is natural in business. So we must look at how we react when our employees bring anything to us. Employees need to have confidence in management. Managers and leaders must understand that if we in any way make our employees feel uncomfortable by our reaction, then we will lose that confidence. Employees will become hesitant and may stop bringing issues to us at all.

"But as we show we are truly open to anything our employees may bring, and if we do not react in a negative manner, they will come forward. When we respond in a calm manner, we can better grasp the entire situation by listening and asking questions. This in turn effects a better suited response.

"If an employee fears belittlement or scrutiny, they convince themselves that there will be no help from management. Employees need to know that any issue they bring is also important to us. We demonstrate this by responding and not forgetting about the issue or diminishing the issue in any way. If my management staff cannot handle the situation, employees know that they are welcome to bring the situation to me. I must lead by example. I work to serve my employees, much like a servant. We must serve our employees."

Again, I was impressed. "Employees can bring situations to you if they are not receiving follow up?"

"Yes. This trains my employees and my managers. Employees will go to where they can get quick results. If any manager does not respond, follow up, or support, my employees know I will. Like I stated before, we must show that we work and serve our employees, not the other way around. This is a true key for a successful manager."

"It actually sounds pretty simple."

"It is. That is the funny thing, the simplicity of it. It is when we overcomplicate things that it becomes difficult. I try to continually ask myself, and now I ask you, what would you desire in an employer? In addition, what environment would you desire to work in?"

I quickly gave my answer: "I would desire an employer who would ask me each day how they could help me, and they genuinely meant it. I want an employer who I trusted would follow up on anything that I bring to them, and I want an employer who supports me, and helps me, by reacting to anything that I bring them in a positive way."

I paused. "Mr. Scott, can I ask how does believing you are servants to your employees affect your managers?"

Mr. Scott stated, "Human nature teaches us to go to where we get results. Managers with big egos and arrogance may fight a "servant" mentality at first, but as success comes, and a healthy environment develops, it breeds itself. Success is our ultimate convincer. We all want results, to drive business, and add growth. Good managers learn that this way of functioning creates success for all."

"Where did you develop this method?"

"I didn't develop it. I learned it from experience." Mr. Scott smiled. "This method, or any other methods or beliefs that you will witness here, have been out in society for everyone. It is very simple to put into perspective. Always ask yourself, 'What would be ideal for you'? Then execute the same for your employees."

"Execute?"

"Too many times we as managers list and demand our expectations of others. We tell employees and management staff, 'This is what I expect.' Yet we don't live up to those expectations in return. Our employees will watch us and will follow us. If I expect something, I simply give it and live it. Then and only then will it become the normal process for everyone. It becomes infectious. Employees begin to take pride and ownership of the environment. It is similar to the example in marriage. In marriage, if you desire more affection, don't demand it, simply just give it. You will be surprised on how easy it is."

"Wonderful," I said, beginning to see why Mr. Scott was so respected. "Now can you tell me about the next sign "Rewards or Consequences"?"

Mr. Scott leaned back in his chair and replied, "In everything we do, there are consequences. Everything we do creates a result. Our actions define what that result will be. But what defines our actions are our behaviors. If we exhibit the correct behavior, our actions will follow suit. With correct actions, our results are more likely to be what is desired.

"From a management perspective, the earlier we can define and correct bad behaviors and actions, the quicker we can develop better results. This is where rewards or consequences comes in play. We inform all employees that we use a system of rewards and consequences. When desired behavior and actions are exhibited, we reward it. When incorrect or non-desired behavior is exhibited, then that employee will have consequences.

"Rewards come in many different facets such as compliments, recognition, key accounts, time off, bonuses, promotions, etc. More importantly, we clearly show that those operating continually on the rewards side are the ones that grow into success with management support. On the other side, consequences bring confrontation and behavior modification. We address the behavior and any issues relating to it. The employee will clearly see that they do not benefit by using incorrect behavior and receive management attention and assistance.

"We all know employers who say, 'My way or the highway.' They try to implement this by demand, force, screaming, and many other methods. We simply reward what is being done right. It is visual and effective. Whatever behavior I desire, I simply have to reward it openly. It is known to all that there are consequences for incorrect behavior and actions."

I nodded. "So how do you work with someone who needs to face the consequence side?"

"Certainly anyone facing consequences I try to convert to the reward side. I define and explain exactly what I am doing to the individual and what I expect. I owe this to their success. So when an employee exhibits incorrect behaviors, actions or results, they must face a consequence. Our goal is to correct behavior before that behavior becomes a bad result. But the importance is that they face a consequence that defines clearly that there are consequences for incorrect behavior, actions and results."

"Yes," I agreed. "You reward good behavior and try to correct any incorrect behavior before it leads to wrong actions. So how do you recognize bad behavior, and how do you correct it?"

"Here is a common example," Mr. Scott replied. "Imagine an employee that is prepared and ready to start the work day at 8:00a.m. He arrives on time, he is organized and he follows a plan. His actions are demonstrating good behavior, correct?"

I shook my head in agreement.

"Next we start to witness that employee become less prepared and he is barely arriving on time, maybe even late, and not having planned like before. That lack of timeliness is the action driving his behavior. Many times an employee's behavior or actions do not show a bad result immediately. This creates a false sense of security and will be harmful and delay management's reaction and correction. Many times the employee may still be producing good results, but soon these incorrect behaviors and actions bring bad results. Sometimes the employee will mask the warning signs that management could have seen."

"So what do you do to prevent that from occurring?"

"It is important to set principles that clearly define in what I call black and white terms what incorrect behavior and actions are for all employees. This will demonstrate that regardless of the employee, bad behavior is the same for each. This allows you to recognize bad behavior and react quickly. This is a hard-set principle that you must establish that allows you to recognize it. I caution and coach all management on this process. As managers, it is easy to overlook bad behaviors on a high-producing employee because of their production and because it takes a while for their behavior and actions to change their results. Establishing the black and white principle help eliminates that from occurring because you will see the warning signs."

"What happens if managers catch bad behavior and ignore it?"

"If a person is not held accountable, then you have actually done them a disservice. After all, we know that bad behavior brings bad results. So it is imperative that everyone knows the process of rewards or consequence. As children, most of us had responsibilities around the house that we were expected to do along with the expectation to do well in school. If we failed in these responsibilities, we then faced consequences. The problem arises when parents warn of consequences and then do not follow through. The person deserving of consequences may even say that they'll not do it again or that they understand. But because of having no consequences, they have not suffered. It is this process that corrects behavior. The lack of this process breeds more bad behavior. Human nature teaches us that we got away with something. Others that witness this will feel the same way and realize that the consequence for bad behavior is not a big concern. You'll breed a bad environment."

"So with consequences, how can you breed a good environment?"

"Number one is to let everyone know about rewards or consequences from day one. Educate and communicate exactly what you mean. Number two, define as much as possible the black and white process of bad behavior, actions, and results. Once again, educate and communicate. Number three, always have a consequence. Number four, after defining and assessing the consequence, implement with complete follow through. Do not let up halfway through the process. As managers, we need to show consistency, integrity, and that we follow through."

"What if one of your managers assesses punishment on an employee that is too severe or unfair in your point of view?" I asked.

"Well, as I groom my managers, we assess a consequence together, which enables them to learn from me. Now no matter what stage they are in management, they can always consult with me, as many do. But even after these scenarios, if I assess one I believe is too severe, or I disagree with, I will usually honor their assessment, but I will educate them on my beliefs and my point of view. However, what we are talking about is delegation. The true definition of delegation is the giving of responsibility to those that are ready. For the most part, our managers will be ready when they are given this responsibility. But on the rare occasions a consequence was too extreme, then we must show humility, correct the consequence with balance, and we must be honest about the situation. Humility allows us to call things what they are, a mistake. Employees would rather you make a correction and be honest, than be stubborn and prideful. Humility earns respect. With that said, I find that as I lead by example, most situations on behavior correction are consistent and with no surprises."

"Are there other factors taken into account when assessing consequences?"

"Most definitely there are other factors. This part is not black and white. It is more a process of looking at the incorrect behavior, action, or result, and balancing it with the employees' development stage. Some bad behaviors are common sense. I expect more from an employee that has been with us for a year than one that has been with us for a week. I also have higher expectations for my leaders and my managers. These are the factors that we take into consideration. The question that you must ask when making your decision on consequence is 'What can I do to correct this behavior, action, or result, along with educating and advancing the employee?' That is what it is about, the betterment of all.

"Consequences are just accountability. Accountability is how each of us learns in life and in society. In society we have laws established, and we know that breaking a law will bring consequences. A failure to face those consequences, or a sense that we got away with something, will breed more bad behavior. When bad behavior is not corrected, more bad behavior will breed itself. This works in families, society, and in business.

"I was recently watching a television sitcom. The husband and wife were debating over punishment they had imposed on their daughter for her bad behavior. They grounded her for a period of time. The father was having second thoughts and was attempting to talk his wife into lifting the consequence and allowing the daughter to go out. The wife simply stated that she believed it was important to follow through on the consequence so any future thoughts of bad behavior by the daughter would be avoided, as they were surely laying the foundation of consistency and completeness. Second, the wife believed that by lifting the consequence before its fruition would send a bad message to their daughter and create a discipline problem in the future. The same applies to the workplace. An employer is being observed by all other employees. Simply stated, we must always assign a consequence and always follow through."

I enjoyed Mr. Scott's thoroughness. I asked, "What about employees who exhibited the same bad behavior yet received different consequences? How do you explain that?"

"That is a good question. That is the why you need black and white terms and consistency in assigning a consequence. Now what may differ is the severity of the consequence. It is subjective based upon what stage of accountability the employee is in, and what factors are involved. Newer employees may differ from those of longer tenure. Naturally, if you are dealing with a persistent problem compared to another employee's first occurrence, then that consideration will then determine proper consequences. We do this in our society by allowing judges and juries to assess punishment in criminal trials. Decisions are based upon past history, as well as the nature of the crime. In business, it is done very much in the same manner.

"When I assess a consequence, I communicate how I determined that consequence and I define expectations of corrective action. I teach this to our management staff. It is important that we utilize consequences as a tool."

"I see." I said. "It is about taking responsibility, both employees and management. Management must properly assess consequences and employees must modify their behavior to that which gets rewards."

"Exactly," Mr. Scott replied. "When an individual takes responsibility, they learn from their behavior."

"And those that do not take responsibility?" I asked.

"Well, we see it all the time, don't we? Some individuals believe they are being singled out unfairly. They blame others or some other factors. To prevent this, we try to be consistent in our approach. We are quick to respond to all situations, good and bad. Employees will observe our consistency. When we institute consequences, we educate and coach the employee through the process. It is imperative not to humiliate or belittle the individual. It is an opportunity to teach from the behavior that needs correcting.

"You witness employees' openness and responsiveness, or lack thereof. Individuals who fail at assuming responsibility are generally consistent about it as it has become a normal behavior. Their behavior drives their action, which defines the result. So we clearly define to each employee what we are doing with rewards or consequence, and we explain why. The quicker an individual takes responsibility then the more open they become to learning and listening. Finally, they become more open to correction. I assist and teach each employee with every bit of my patience, understanding, and effort. My management staff does the same. We realize that the behaviors of others are impacted by witnessing this process. My desire, or shall I say our desire, is for each employee to have trust and confidence in their entire management staff."

Mr. Scott pointed in the direction of his sales floor. "95% of our sales staff arrive around 7:30am, but our start time is actually 8am. I do not require our employees to be here early, but I expect them to be as prepared as possible by 8am so they can take full advantage of their day. Obviously I point out how it increases their productivity, their organization, and all other things that drive success. Employees that are ready and working when 8am rolls around are rewarded with my personal time, effort, and attention. More importantly, I lead by example, as I arrive early to be available and helpful. It has become a good time for employees to ask for my help, advice, opinions, and coaching. I make it a point to be accessible."

"What is the behavior of those who do not give 100% at 8am?" I was intrigued.

"They are the ones getting coffee, chit-chatting, and mostly doing nonproductive things. An honest day's work is being ready when the time that you are paid for begins. Those that give that effort by their behavior and action find rewards. Take Eugene as an example. He is one of our top sales representatives and is an excellent multi-tasker and a very organized employee. Eugene arrives early on most occasions. Eugene truly works hard on his productivity, and his success shows it."

"How do you reward?"

"We use rewards in many different ways. It doesn't have to be monetary, although it can be. Many times it's extra positive attention by me or our staff. We give energy and time with that employee. This attention helps them overall in their career. I can reward them with additional clients and opportunities. Ultimately it is the employees' success that grows. Other employees witness this process and results, and they desire the same thing. Eugene and most of the staff are here early because they enjoy the benefits of that time and they are continually growing in their careers."

"So what are other benefits?"

"Well, there is a big one for management."

"Please explain."

"With rewards and consequences, management sees which individuals we need to focus our attention on. I desire our staff to spend our energy and time with the employees that are teachable. My definition of teachable is employees that respond to our coaching, and truly desire success, and are open minded. Shouldn't that employee deserve my effort?"

"Sure," I said, "but do other employees then fail?"

"Sometimes they do. But hopefully their behavior changes to our desired behavior. I make it very clear that I play favorites. I play favorites to those who honestly desire my help and energy by giving the desired behavior."

"How do they respond to you playing favorites?"

"Some are surprised at first. But I explain why I do it. All employees have this knowledge up front, so they have no complaint later. Playing favorites is not based on anything discriminatory like race, sex, etc. Playing favorites is based on behavior and effort."

I had to admit this was fair, reasonable and logical.

"Now would be a good time to explain what I call the reward or consequences teeter-totter," Mr. Scott said.

"Teeter-totter?" I asked. "Like on a playground?"

"Yes. Let me show you from this diagram." Mr. Scott then pulled out two drawings from a folder he had sitting on his desk and laid each one before me.

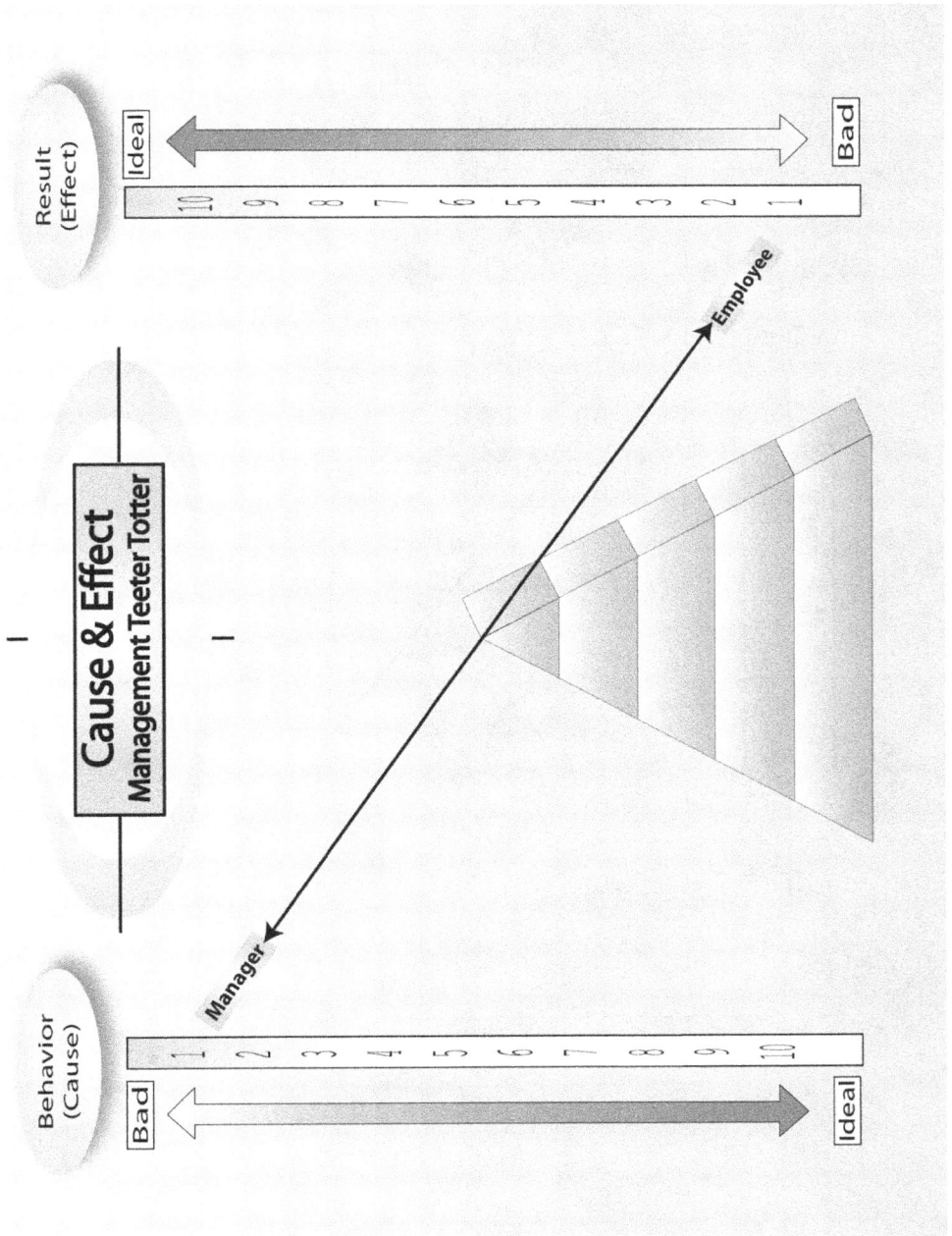

Cause & Effect
Management Teeter Totter

Result (Effect)
Ideal
10 9 8 7 6 5 4 3 2 1
Bad

Behavior (Cause)
Bad
1 2 3 4 5 6 7 8 9 10
Ideal

Manager

Employee

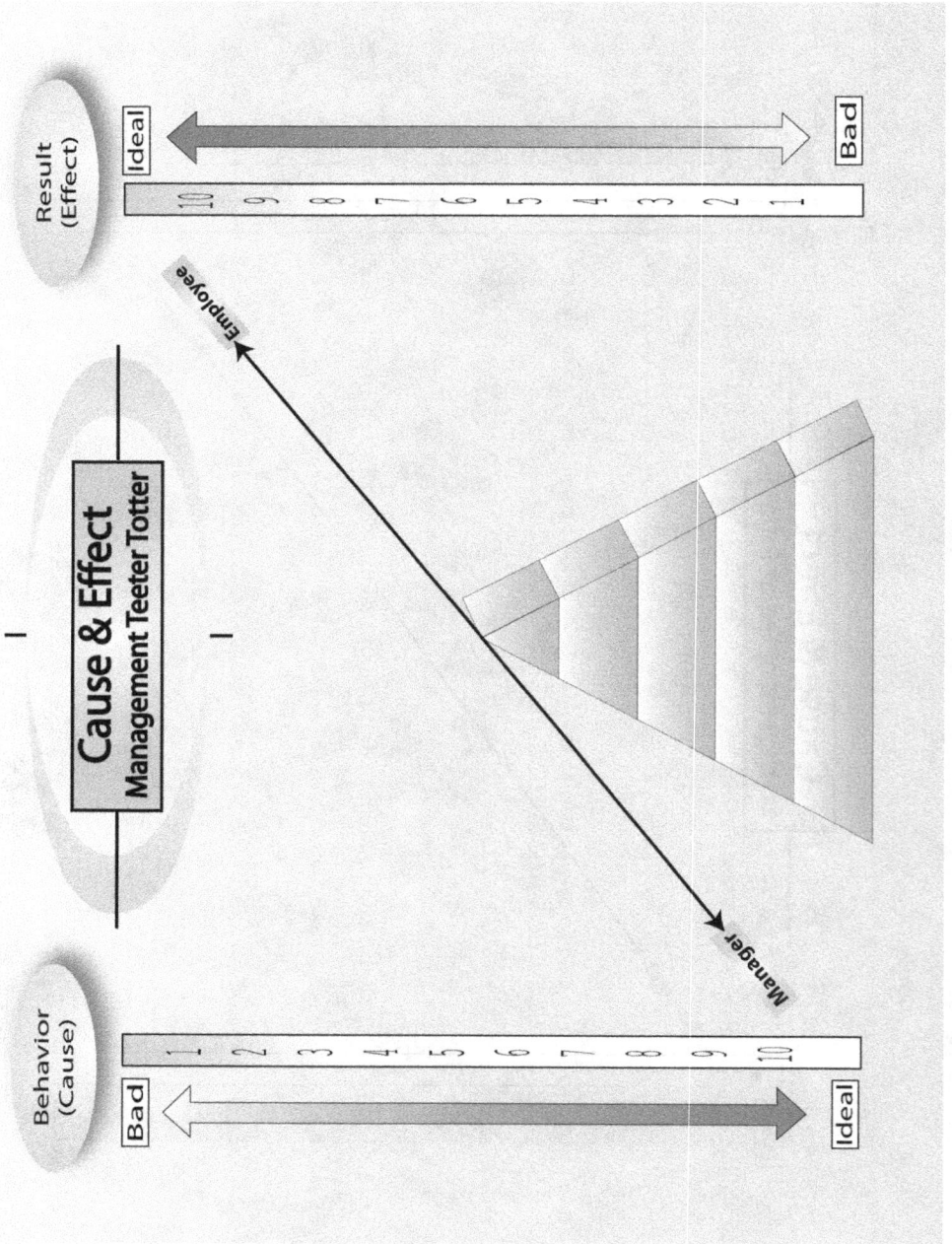

Cause & Effect
Management Teeter Totter

Result (Effect)

Ideal

Bad

10 9 8 7 6 5 4 3 2 1

Employee

Manager

Behavior (Cause)

Bad

Ideal

1 2 3 4 5 6 7 8 9 10

"First, let me give you an explanation by using a parent and a child. When that parent takes their child to a playground, their obvious desire is for their child to be safe and have fun. When both are accomplished, they have achieved their desired result. A child that has a good, safe, fun day grows up in a healthy environment. The parent and child both use their energy in achieving this result. If the child exhibits good behavior, it is more than likely that all was safe and fun. But if that child exhibits bad behavior by misusing a playground toy, the child can get hurt, which is the consequence of that behavior. At that time, the parent has to then focus on the result that occurred and help their injured child. The whole focus and desired result of the day are gone and has even added more distractions and has drawn added attention."

"Yeah, the whole idea of a fun day at the playground is lost."

"Exactly, but let's take a step back. As that child started to exhibit bad behavior, the parent could correct the child's behavior and instruct the child on the proper use of that playground toy. The parent could correct them back to good behavior. The parent does this knowing bad behavior will cause bad consequences. They correct behavior quickly and as often as needed."

"Sure. If not, the child could get hurt," I agreed.

"Yes, but the child doesn't realize that factor. The child is ignorant to that fact. The parent corrects the behavior in the best interest of the child. It is obvious that what is best for the child is best also for the parent, right?"

"Of course." I replied.

"Correct the behavior quickly and then concentrate on good behavior so the child will not see the bad results. By correcting the bad behavior, the parents will then redirect their focus on rewarding good behavior. With their energy focused properly, the ideal result will come naturally."

"It seems to make sense."

"Sure it does. But in business most employers tend to wait for the bad results to occur. Then the focus is spent on correcting the results. This takes a lot of time and energy. We find it wiser to correct the behavior that is driving the final result before a bad result occurs. If our energy is refocused on a good behavior, then we are likely to see a better or ideal result."

I agreed. "It seems pretty easy to understand. Can you explain the significance of these drawings of the teeter-totters?"

"Sure. Let's look at chart #1. Our staff's focus is where they allow their energy to be based on the teeter-totter. The employee sits on the opposite side of the manager. So where we as managers focus our time and energy on is where more weight is given. This weight and energy drives the employee on the other end or we allow the employees results to drive us. As you observe the chart, the scale on the left hand side, which is the behavior side, you will see bad behavior being at the top of the scale with good behavior on the bottom. Good behavior or ideal behavior is a 10 on the scale, and as you are driven up, the scale goes to number 1 or bad behavior. Now on the right hand side, you'll notice this is the consequence side or the results. On the result side, you will see ideal consequence at the top of the scale as a number 10 and bad consequence or result being at the bottom as a number 1. If we as managers allow the employee's bad results to drive us, the lack of focus this creates keeps that employee in their bad behaviors. But, on Teeter Totter #2, you'll see that if our focus as managers is on driving good behavior by rewards, correction, coaching, and teaching, then our energy is being utilized correctly and this will keep our employees enjoying and benefiting the ideal results."

"And I would bet they would be having fun also?"

"Sure they are! And we desire them to have fun. But we as managers must drive it from the behavior side."

"Every business has to deal with bad results from time to time. So at that time, what do you do?" I asked.

"We obviously must work on the result, but we quickly correct the behavior or eliminate it. It is imperative that our focus stays on good behavior. Consistency and being involved is the key. You quickly determine as a manager whether the employee comprehends. You define whether they are teachable, coachable, and worth your energy. We give them the benefit of our time by coaching and correcting, and it does not take long to determine if the employee can change their behavior."

"So what happens then?"

"We understand that if the employee's behavior cannot be corrected, they will consume management's focus and attention. The behavior must change to good behavior or we must eliminate the cause, which would be the employee. I have seen too many managers hang on to employees whose behavior was not changing to good behavior, and management would then spend too much focus and energy trying to make that employee successful. The more energy spent with that employee, the less energy there is for employees exhibiting good behavior. Eventually this starts hurting other areas. You will also find it takes more energy to focus on bad behavior than on good behavior."

"How is that so?"

"I'll explain. Let's go back to the parent with the child on the playground. Suppose the child's bad behavior results in a bad result, an injury. The parent's anxiety increases with the stress of the situation. The parent then has to attend to the injury or even go to a doctor. The bad behavior that brought the bad result has now cost that parent added time and energy on things that the parent had not planned on. With good behavior, the bad results never occur, therefore, conserving energy."

"I understand. So what helps keep that child in good behavior?"

"Simple," Mr. Scott said. "The parent will use rewards or consequences. As long as that child is in good behavior, they should be rewarded with things like their parents' involvement or maybe extra playtime. If bad behavior brings a bad result, like an injury, that injury is a bad consequence in itself. But that parent still must give that child a consequence. A consequence could be taking away playtime in the future, etc. What is important is the parents' involvement. The more the parent participates with the child, the more that child enjoys their day. The more active that parent is, the more aware that parent is. Managing employees works the same."

"When you explain it like that, it sounds so reasonable. Thank you for all of this discussion. So now, finally, tell me about cause and effect."

"Sure," Mr. Scott replied. "Everything we discussed is part of cause and effect, but there is much more."

"How is that?"

"Well, you'll get a clearer picture when you'll visit with our management staff and employees. But let me give you a quick breakdown of cause and effect. For every final result, there were behaviors that brought actions which culminated in that final result. So we make our focus on that behavior or what is otherwise known as the cause, trusting that we will bring about the ideal result, which is the effect.

"Now when a bad or negative result occurs, we define what was the cause that culminated in that result? What was the behavior? We can then make our corrections. Many times it came about by a little change in DNA, so we ended up with a frog instead of a prince as we discussed earlier. An effect is brought about by cause or causes. In science, a scientist will look at an effect or result, and work backwards to define a cause. Science defined that the Grand Canyon, an effect, was caused by the Colorado River. No river, no Grand Canyon. In business, we define and determine good effects and then define what behaviors bring about those desired effects.

"By determining the causes, we then can focus our training and our environment to be conducive to developing good behaviors. Now we also define incorrect or bad causes. By determining incorrect or bad behaviors or actions, we can work to recognize such behaviors early in the process to avoid bad effects. Correcting at the behavior stage is much easier than waiting for the fruition of their effects. Through experience and continual learning, we define what good behavior is and what bad behavior is. Experience is learned as we deal with successes and failures and define the causes for each."

"So you're stating that you can avoid bad effects by early intervention? In a sense, you're altering future bad effects and changing them to good or desired results?" I asked.

"Absolutely! Many historians ponder on historical issues such as past wars or such tragic examples like the holocaust. We have all heard the statement of people saying to themselves, 'If I only knew then what I know now.' Our history lessons define what the causes of such events were. In fact, there have been many books, shows, and movies on the subject of the ability to go back in time and change or eliminate those causes, which in effect would change the future results. Well, in business, we do not have to wait on the future, as long as we focus in the early stages of behavior and actions. Correcting behavior is a key to successful results. This is what I call business cause and effect in regard to behavior. Cause and effect does not just relate to behavior. Business structure, systems, development, and budgetary changes all need to consider cause and effect."

"I see you place emphasis on being open and honest about causes," I stated.

"We learn from the experience. Personally, I try to show that when I make an error, I admit it, accept it, take responsibility, and move forward, setting the focus on correcting the right behavior and action. I treat every situation like I would like to be treated and corrected. This is the consistency we strive to show. I desire that all of us learn and advance from the situation. Our job is the success and health of our business. We as managers owe it to all of our employees to operate a profitable, stable, and successful business. I, as the top manager of this location, make sure this is known. I not only announce this fact, but I strive to show it daily. Humility allows us to be open-minded and learn from employees as much as they learn from us. Look, people like success. Grow their success and you will gain loyalty. Success becomes infectious to other employees and drives excitement."

"It does sound like an ideal environment, but are there any draw-backs?"

"Sure, there can be. Do not let cause and effect philosophies become an excuse, and it will become a way of life."

"Can you please explain?"

Mr. Scott paused for a moment, and then he replied. "Well, it ties into follow-up, support, and reaction. I desire for our employees to have quick answers and solutions as much as possible. I have witnessed managers use the excuse of 'still thinking on it' and they delay or don't respond. This frustrates our employees, and we lose their trust and confidence."

"So how do you find balance?" I asked.

"When I train a new manager, I monitor that manager carefully. I welcome managers to utilize me, with no embarrassment or judgment. I make sure it is known that I am available always. They can bring anything to me. It is very important that our employees get quick and timely responses, and that they know I am available. As I stated before, I desire employees and managers to know this fact. So if a manager cannot resolve a situation or circumstance, they will bring it to me. This also helps me manage my managers. I encourage this behavior by rewarding this behavior. If a manager's answer to an employee was not ideal in any way, I coach and teach what would have been ideal. We all learn from the experience."

"Okay, so this way of operating becomes a way of life?" I queried.

"Well," Mr. Scott answered, "the more you practice cause and effect, the more it becomes natural. Your thought process will sharpen with your focus. Soon it becomes natural with the repetition of your focus and practice. I compare it to learning to ride a bike. When you are first learning, you have someone assisting you, coaching you, reminding you of each thing to do. Your mind focuses on each of the instructions. You remember each one. Soon you are riding by yourself, with no apprehension. After a while, you will simply jump on the bike without any thought, as it has become second nature. It happened because of the continual practice."

"Is there anything else you want to share?" I was grateful for the time Mr. Scott had been spending with me.

"Yes, keep it simple. I know we have all heard that said many times. But truly we need to keep things simple and not overcomplicate them. Cause and effect will draw your focus to basic fundamentals of your business. That is why I like it so much."

"Can you explain more?"

"Sure, the basic fundamentals of your business are just like the basic fundamentals in sports. Execution is the first part. We must succeed at execution for our ideal success. For example, in football, the offensive linemen must block for the running back to gain yards. If the offensive linemen do not execute the blocking scheme, the runner has no success. Blocking is a basic fundamental of football. With no execution on blocking and no success for the runner, the final results can be a loss. If not corrected, it can be a losing season. This demoralizes the whole team. But if the behavior is corrected, the behavior of learning and executing the blocking schemes with continual practice, the team can start winning. This is the ideal result. Success creates fun and excitement. Players push each other's behavior and hold each other accountable. That is the ideal environment you're developing. You have your players then taking ownership. So by keeping it simple, you're drawn back to executing the basic fundamentals. Every business has basic fundamentals."

"It sure makes sense. I now see how some football coaches can take over a losing team and have immediate improvement with the same players." I smiled.

"Exactly! The first thing that coach does is to turn his players' focus back to the basic fundamentals and hold his players accountable. Obviously the players are on the team because they exhibited qualities that ownership or prior management desired. They had perceived value. The new coach simply focuses on the basic fundamentals first, usually with no drastic changes, just execution."

"I think I understand, but how is it implemented?"

"First announce to everyone that management will focus on the fundamentals and hold each person accountable. Management will define what their expectations are in regards to desired behavior. Then management will immediately correct behavior using rewards or consequences and work to eliminate bad behavior. Using football as the example, a reward can be a compliment, more playing time in a game, or being promoted and playing with the first string. The key is to be consistent and to continually focus on the basic fundamentals. Managers must always continually communicate what they are doing and what behaviors they desire.

"You then must point to successes. When you have ideal behaviors and results, use it as a tool to show what the positive behavior was and that it was the determining factor for the ideal result to occur.

Managers will see their players, or employees in our case, catch on and do the same. Remember, hold bad behavior accountable for change and coach to what your expectations are."

"Okay, anything else you'd like to add?"

"Yes, point to your model players. Use them as leaders. Remember, your model players must be exhibiting the behavior you desire."

"Sure, is there any reason why they would not be?"

"Well, let me explain. You may have a player who may have had some success, but does not exhibit your desired behavior. Usually their success is short-lived and they will have to change their behavior to your desired behavior or fail. A coach would want their players looking at someone like Walter Payton was for the Chicago Bears."

"Sure, Walter Payton was so naturally talented."

"He was, and he was a humble man. Because of his humility, Walter Payton was determined not to rely on just his natural talents. I ask you, do you think Walter Payton understood blocking schemes and how to follow them?"

"Absolutely, that is what made him such a great runner."

"Yes, but Walter Payton always studied and practiced the fundamentals. He studied weekly films and each week's game plan. Payton never said, 'I already know this stuff.' He studied because he wanted continued success. Look at the longevity of his career. A coach wants his players modeling that attitude and behavior. That type of leader is invaluable."

I shook my head in agreement. "I like that analogy. Now previously you mentioned to 'announce it.' I believe I understand, but can you expand on it some more?"

"Sure, but I will use baseball as an example this time. Let's start by me asking you a question. Do you believe coaches want to win the next game?"

"Of course, that should be obvious."

"It should be. I know my employees want to close business and be successful. But to take it further, should not the coaches' ideal result be to win consistently, which creates a winning season and ultimately a championship?"

"I would think so. I mean, isn't this a no-brainer?"

"Sure it is. Just as my ideal results are for our employees to close business consistently, and continually, along with building repeat business consistently from satisfied clients."

"Yes, client retention is a key. But can you go back to your example?"

"Okay, let's say that a baseball team is preparing for their next game. We know, of course, that they want to win. But what if the coach tells his team, 'Okay, team, this game I want to win by the score of 5 to 3 with us making a comeback in the bottom of the ninth'?"

"I would think that would confuse his players."

"It absolutely would, but there are many business managers that do just that. They focus on a grand result instead of the fundamentals of success that will lead to great results. A baseball coach focuses on basic fundamental behaviors that would make the team play better baseball, which ultimately develops a winning team. The coach and staff focus on hitting, fielding, basic running, pitching, etc. The players will learn and also focus on the scouting report on the next team they play. This will allow them to work on the execution of those behaviors. Managers can focus on the fundamentals of their team and let that create the winning results."

"Simple enough, I believe I have a general understanding of cause and effect. What can I expect to learn by visiting your management staff and employees?" I was ready to meet with others now.

"Execution," Mr. Scott said. "You have learned basic concepts, now go see it in action."

Mr. Scott pulled out an organizational chart depicting each manager listed by title and duties. Each employee was listed under each manager of their department in a flowchart format. Mr. Scott gave a brief explanation of each department, highlighting department responsibilities and objectives. He encouraged me to ask candid questions and assured me of his staff's openness.

"Mr. Scott," I said, "Thank you for your time this morning and your insight. Can we meet at the end of the day for more conversation?"

"Absolutely, that was going to be my suggestion. I can answer any additional questions you may have at that time. Plus, I would also value your insight and observations."

"Thank you. Before I visit your staff, are there any pearls of wisdom you would like to leave me with?"

Mr. Scott laughed, then said while still laughing, "Yes, crap or honey?"

I must have looked dumbfounded and confused. "Pardon me?"

"I apologize," he said. Mr. Scott pointed to a sign only visible from his side of the desk.

"Crap or Honey is a reminder to be cognizant how I lead and manage."

"Why do you have that sign where only you can see it?"

"For one, I don't wish to offend anyone with the word crap. But also, it is a reminder to me that how I lead as a manager is very important."

"Can you further explain?"

"Yes, it is actually very simple. Both crap or honey roll downhill, or in the case of honey, it may ooze downhill slowly, but you understand the picture."

I replied, "Yes, they both make their way downhill, but I am still confused. Can you explain more?"

Mr. Scott responded, "Whatever is on top of a hill makes its way down and affects what is below. So if you have crap on top, you will get crap below. If you have honey on top, you will get honey below. As this location's manager, I must always remember the effect I have. It is very important for me to be aware how I manage, how I am received, and how I respond. I desire to exhibit good qualities that are positive to roll downhill. Affecting my staff and employees in a positive way is imperative. I desire to be a benefit to my employees."

"I understand. Mr. Scott, from our conversation to this point, if I asked you for four key points for me to take away, what would they be?"

Mr. Scott paused and then replied, "Number one, be genuine and open-minded and accessible to all your employees. Number two, make it known immediately to all employees that you play favorites and why; then do so consistently. Number three, exhibit by example the behavior you desire and expect. Number four, exhibit humility and demonstrate through action that you work for your employees."

"Thank you, Mr. Scott." I shook his hand as we stood up. "Can you point me in the direction of Mr. Douglas? According to your organizational chart, he is your recruiter. I believe he will be my next meeting, if that's fine with you?"

"Good choice." Mr. Scott then proceeded to walk me over to Mr. Douglas's cubicle.

Chapter Two

THE HEART OF THE PROBLEM[1]

Mr. Douglas appeared to be in his thirties, was well-groomed and well-dressed, and kept his work area well organized. I noticed a picture on his desk of a lovely woman with two little boys. "I assume this is your family?" I asked.

"Sure is," he answered with a big smile.

"You are a lucky man," I replied.

"Thank you. Yes, I know," he responded.

As he tidied some paperwork, I noticed he had a list of five monthly goals and a list of five annual goals hanging up in his cubicle. I also took note of four computer-printed signs he had posted. The first read, "Everyone is a 10." The second sign said, "Factual, not negative." The third sign stated, "Trust yet verified", and the fourth sign, "Short-cuts get you lost!"

"I appreciate your time," I said. "I am very interested in your hiring practices and your philosophies."

"Okay, shoot." Mr. Douglas leaned back in his chair.

"Do you currently have any openings?" I asked.

"I have a few," he said. "I have room for a couple of sales representatives, an opening in our service side and one in our receptionist side
at night."

"Are they considered big needs?" I asked.

"Well," he said, "I never take hiring lightly. Whether we need one
employee or twenty, who we add to our team must be a fit and share
our vision. Our sales staff is stable at the present time, but we always
stay active in recruiting. This adds to our success.

"It is our philosophy that we owe it to our employees to always look
for other good employees in all areas. Sometimes it is when you believe
that you are at an okay state that you will miss your best candidates. If
we continually look, we will continue to function at a high level. Also,
in a strange yet positive way, it keeps the current staff motivated."

"How is that?" I asked. "Aren't your employees then looking over
their shoulders?"

"Let me explain it like this," Mr. Douglas replied. "First, we make
no secret of our continued efforts to recruit. We clearly explain that
we always desire the best staff. We believe and understand that our
employees desire the same. Wouldn't you want to work for a company that continually strives to have the most productive and efficient
employees driving that company's success? Is it not also our responsibility to provide the highest potential of success for the company to
maintain stability for our employees?"

"It makes sense to me," I said, "but I ask once more. Don't some
employees look over their shoulders?"

"Look," he said, "I want employees with confidence, initiative, and
direction. We clearly define expectations, and each employee will always
know where they stand. If I have someone looking over their shoulder
worried about keeping their job, that is their issue. It is our responsibility as managers to be direct and honest on employee performance. If

someone is needlessly looking over their shoulder, we will refocus them and encourage them. But those that may warrant that perception are only exhibiting a behavior of their concern and attitude. We will give them every benefit of counsel, training, and time. But someone continually looking over their shoulder may be exhibiting a final behavior of giving up. So this actually works to us as an indication."

"I understand," I replied, "I guess as long as you communicate your policy and why."

"We do," he said. "I have worked in environments where management did not communicate. Our staff knows and believes that knowledgeable employees will understand our philosophy and have buy-in. We do our employees a service by eliminating any surprises. Let me ask you a question, do you like sports?"

"Yes," I said. "I enjoy watching them, more than playing them."

"Well," he replied, "don't the best sport teams always look for good players, even after they may have won the championship?"

"Yes," I said, "I guess so."

"They sure do," he replied. "They know that for their team to stay on top, they must always keep their eyes open for good players. Our company is no different. If we do what is in the best interest of our company and our clients and stay successful as we serve them, our employees benefit from a stable company. So our first philosophy is to always be looking for good employees, no matter what our status may be at the moment. What good sports team would turn down a good player who is available? Sometimes the good teams will find ways to work it out, and sometimes they must make difficult decisions, but we owe it to our clients and our employees to add good players when available."

"The philosophy sounds good," I said. "With your demographics, do you find it easier to hire trained people? Would they need less supervision?"

The smile left Mr. Douglas's face. He scooted his chair a little closer to mine and said, "That is the heart of the problem.[2] The self-managed employee does not exist. To believe that they do will waste your time in hiring and training. Sure, some demographic areas may have more qualified candidates, but I have seen good employees come from all demographics. We must first understand that everyone needs managing. Everyone needs behavior modification. An employee that lacks supervision and behavior modification will lack motivation and direction and will fail. It is natural human nature that all people will crave and flourish when they receive both direction and motivation that comes from coaching. That coaching only comes from supervision and behavior modification. Hiring the best candidate to fit this criterion will help, but realizing the heart of the problem will make you hire better. I know it has helped me as a recruiter and as a trainer."

"How would that be?"

"Well," he said, "I once believed that you could hire the self-managed person. I had candidates I considered close to this model, but eventually they failed. Looking back, I blame myself, as I can now see where they started to stray and I did not correct them. I once complained to my old boss by saying, 'They're adults. Why don't they do what they are paid for?' Eventually I learned that had I kept up with behavior modification through rewards or consequences, many of the past employees would probably be here today. I now understand that I failed them as their manager. I have made it a point to learn from that."

"What were some of the things that helped you learn this?"

Mr. Douglas replied, "Our employee turnover was continually high. We were having some success as a business, and we accepted that high turnover went with the territory. But I would often get frustrated because we would have very good prospects who seemed to catch on, then eventually would stray from good behavior of execution; some quickly, others gradually. We as managers would get frustrated and show it in how we tried to correct and confront our employees. We lost many good employees that might have succeeded."

"How did you develop the change in philosophy?" I asked.

"It wasn't easy," he replied. "Actually I fought it at first. When Mr. Scott first took over, he met with all employees and explained his beliefs and style. He then met with me individually, as he did all managers, and reviewed my hiring and training process. Mr. Scott explained how he would participate in the process of hiring and recruiting. He explained his philosophy of how the initial recruiting and hiring was the most important investment that we make as a business."

"So at which point did you fight it?" I asked

"At the very beginning. Although what Mr. Scott said made sense, I was blind to the facts. Actually my pride was a barrier. I felt Mr. Scott simply did not trust my hiring. I actually took the same attitude about our employees. My belief was, 'I'm an adult, and I can be trusted with the hiring.' Even a part of me said to myself that I was doing fine until Mr. Scott arrived."

"How did the change come about?"

"Simple," he answered. "Mr. Scott's follow-through was thorough. When he asked me to notify him about our schedule of hiring events or interviews, if I did not answer, he followed up. I hired a couple of employees my old way and it did not get past Mr. Scott. I laugh about it now, but this is where I learned the valuable tool of the rehire technique."

"The rehire technique?" I asked.

Mr. Douglas was smiling again. "It is a great and effective technique used to draw the line with an employee, in no uncertain terms, which will either gain buy-in from the employee or determine the job is not for them."

"Interesting," I said. "Tell me more."

"Sure," he said. "I realized Mr. Scott's follow-through was very thorough yet I also took this as not trusting me. I never saw Mr. Scott get upset. He would simply ask about our scheduled events. I would tell him that I already did a hiring event. Mr. Scott would reply, 'Mr. Douglas, it is imperative that I be involved in our hiring events, interviews, and the hiring decisions.' He would then inform me of when to schedule the next event. There became no way for me to avoid Mr. Scott's process. I did not realize at the time that he was using rewards or consequences on me. I just knew I did not like the consequences each time he followed up with me. Soon, Mr. Scott asked me into his office and confronted the situation."

"What did he do?"

"He was very matter of fact. He did not belittle or attack me negatively. Mr. Scott simply stated the facts of the matter. He addressed me with respect but was straightforward. He said, 'Mr. Douglas, I have a problem.' He then detailed how he had asked me to do certain things in which I did not execute. He explained how it made him feel and how it would affect our environment for the worse. He questioned if that was my desire. He was very factual about the matter."

"And what was your reply?"

"I told him I desired a good working relationship with him. I told him I did not believe in his process or the need for his involvement. I stated I handled things fine before his arrival. Mr. Scott allowed for my feedback and explained his reasons, which were very valid. But it came to a point that I was blind to his reasons, and seeing this, it was at this point that Mr. Scott had to draw a line in the sand."

"How did he do that?"

"Very effectively," Mr. Douglas said with a chuckle. "Mr. Scott never raised his voice, which impressed me. He simply looked at me and stated, 'Mr. Douglas, I appreciate your feedback and responses, and I will always appreciate them. However, I believe that we are at a point that I need to readdress the situation. Mr. Douglas, I have a position available. This position is the person who will recruit, hire, and train my employees. This position is an extremely important position as our biggest investment is our employees. This position has such importance that I feel it necessary that I be involved in the process. My process may at times be different than what you may have utilized. I do ask for this position to work closely with me on the hiring process and how I want it executed. I need to ask you, Mr. Douglas, do you want this position?'"

"Wow," I said shaking my head, "that is powerful. How did you respond?"

Mr. Douglas replied, "I really did not have to give it much thought. Mr. Scott was clear and very precise by how he used this technique. I told Mr. Scott I valued my position. I told him I just had some difficulty accepting the changes. Looking back, I remember thinking how professional I thought the approach was. The technique immediately received my buy-in and allowed Mr. Scott and me to open up more on my concerns and his reasoning. My blinders went away. It's funny, but I actually told my wife about what transpired and how I respected Mr. Scott for how he utilized the technique. I was impressed at the simplicity of it."

"It sounds simple," I said. "It really is the old 'This-is-where-the-rubber-meets-the-road speech,' but done in a more effective fashion."

"I agree," Mr. Douglas said. "It received my buy-in in no uncertain terms. There was nothing vague about it. Mr. Scott defined my job description and allowed for my feedback. Then he stated something he had said to all our employees when he was first introduced. He said, 'I need you to understand that although this is your job description, other things may arise that I may ask or have expectations for you to take the initiative in. Each and every job we offer here has a job description. I need you to understand I expect more. Your job comes with pay for the work time you perform. The only thing I will not ask of you is anything that is illegal, immoral, or dishonest. Anything else, I expect it executed and you'll be paid for it.' Given this opportunity with me, he reaffirmed his point. I clearly saw it was his individual opportunity to receive my buy-in."

"So how did he explain this at his original introduction?" I asked.

"Mr. Scott stated that he wanted everyone to realize that although we all have job descriptions, we all do more. He desires employees who take ownership of the business instead of saying, 'That is not my job.' He gave an example of trash on the restroom floor that morning. Apparently he witnessed several employees that had gone in and out of the restroom and the same trash was on the floor after they left. Mr. Scott told us that he simply picked up the trash and threw it away. He pointed out that his job description did not list being a janitor and that we also have a cleaning service, but he believes a clean environment is beneficial to our business. So, Mr. Scott simply picked up the trash and threw it away. He wants us all to understand this issue. I constantly see Mr. Scott doing things that I would clearly say are not in his job description, so he leads by example. The first day he was here, he was cleaning our glass doors to our lobby. I now witness others taking the initiative to do many other tasks.

"I also see where it has become a proactive approach to an employee who has no initiative, and uses his job description as a cop-out. We all have a written and defined job description, but each concludes with the understanding that our jobs may include anything additional we may be asked or expected to do, as long as it is not illegal, immoral, or dishonest. With this, we each accept our positions with this understanding and we know we will be paid in accordance with state and federal laws. We each signed our descriptions and have copies of them."

"Did it bother you at all to sign this?"

"No," he said. "I saw it as buy-in. More and more I see that Mr. Scott is big on communication and buy-in. He tries to eliminate any vagueness or excuses. I see it as motivating. It's funny, but I realize that even like children, we all enjoy and do well in a structured and safe environment. It is very motivating."

I enjoyed Mr. Douglas's tone as he spoke. "So what else can you tell me about the hiring process?" I asked.

Mr. Douglas scratched his head and shrugged his shoulders as if there wasn't much to say, then he stated, "Well, Mr. Scott and I defined goals and the hiring process and standards. Now I see that the most important part of the process is Mr. Scott's involvement. I find this funny because it was what I fought in the beginning. We reviewed our current staff and hiring practices. Mr. Scott did not come in and make major changes. He simply wanted to be a part of the process.

"We reviewed our employee turnover numbers, and although they were high, I believed I was doing a good job. Mr. Scott reiterated I did hire and train good people, but he showed me what turnover really cost, both in salaries and in energy. Mr. Scott pointed out that unfortunately most top managers blame their recruiters for the turnover and do not take ownership or responsibility. I remembered an instance where our last manager did blame me.

"Mr. Scott explained that our employees are the most important investment we make in our business. He told me that my job is a difficult one, and his job is to help me succeed, which benefits us all. He said he has witnessed top managers get upset when they release poor employees and then blame it on their recruiters. Yet those managers took no ownership or responsibility. He helped me see what a poor or lost employee costs us to hire and train, and how managers should take a larger interest in this biggest investment."

Mr. Douglas continued, "I now see why it is so important that Mr. Scott is involved in the process. I see it much like investing in stock. I don't believe most people will give their money blindly to a broker then get upset when the investment turns out bad. Successful individuals are involved in the process of that investment. The stockbroker is there for advice and guidance, but the individual is involved from the beginning and throughout the process. That is how Mr. Scott is with hiring. We have done hiring seminars and individual interviews. Our process is not magically different than other places. What is different is Mr. Scott's involvement. He is involved in how we advertise and recruit, and in what we're looking for in potential employees, the interviewing process, and the final decisions.

"The very thing I fought is now the very thing I love. With Mr. Scott's involvement, he has helped me develop and grow. I am allowed my views and my opinions are appreciated, yet I grow and develop with his insight. Our results are better with our turnover being much lower, and I am reaping the rewards. My job has become very motivating. I can hire more selectively, looking for the right candidate to improve us. We have eliminated hiring out of dire need. So, I have more time to train and follow up on others' progress. I truly enjoy my job."

"I believe you," I said. "I hear it in your voice and I see it in your enthusiasm. Is there anything else that you wish to add on Mr. Scott's involvement?"

"Yes," he said, "Mr. Scott thanks me for the improvement, yet I feel I should thank him. This is what is so motivating. When we had a visit from Mr. Scott's superior, Mr. Scott gave me the credit and the accolades for our improvements and success in this area. Mr. Scott does not pat himself on the back. His attitude drives me to want to be better. I find myself a more loyal employee. These are the things that make me enjoy being employed here. I am more open where I used to be the opposite and protective of my duties. I now see how this environment is much healthier."

"I notice you have some printed signs around your work area, much like Mr. Scott's office," I said. "Can you tell me about them?"

"Sure," Mr. Douglas said, "They are my beliefs and I like constant reminders; and if I make them visible, others will see my values. By this, I am held more accountable."

"Did Mr. Scott require you to do this?" I asked.

"No," he said. "But it was by his example that I did it. I realize we model what we admire and what we desire. I desire to grow and develop in accountability and trust. Mr. Scott lives by the signs in his office. This has earned credibility and trust from all of our employees. To me, it is a valuable tool."

"Your first sign," I said, "says 'Everyone is a 10.' What is your motivation behind it?"

Mr. Douglas replied, "It started in a discussion I had with Mr. Scott about a newer employee having some difficulty catching on. In the conversation I used the word "stupid." Mr. Scott stopped me and shared a principle and belief that is now very important to me. He said, "Mr. Douglas, you, as an individual and as a person, are a ten. No one can take that away from you, nor can anyone take that away from me. Because I am a ten, I will always treat you as a ten. There may be times we disagree and there may be times I am disappointed in you. When these times occur, I will define them as such, but I will still treat you as a ten. I am a ten and you are a ten, we are equal as individuals. Only our employee titles and status may be different. But in our relationship as individuals, I will treat you as an equal because we are both tens. I ask that you treat our employees in the same manner. You are a ten, but so are they. If someone doesn't fit our needs as an employee, that does not make them less of a person.""

"How did you respond?"

"I was embarrassed," Mr. Douglas stated, "but I admit it wasn't uncommon for me to use words like that. Our prior manager commonly used such words or phrases if someone made a mistake or frustrated him. I actually became surprised how it became so common for me to talk like that too."

"How did you and Mr. Scott address it from there?"

"Mr. Scott was very calm, as is his natural demeanor," he said, "but he had a passion about him that flowed through his words. I knew this topic was very important to him. He explained that he deemed it imperative that we treat our employees with respect. He said, 'Mr. Douglas, I am a ten. I know that I am a ten. My superiors can terminate my employment tomorrow and I will still be a ten. I am secure in that. You could call me stupid and it would not have an effect on me, but not everyone has that self-assurance. There are many jobs out there that I am not qualified for, nor capable of doing. If I tried and failed, does that make me less of a person? Of course not. I am still a ten.' His analogy made me realize that someone may not work out as an employee but that does not make them less of a person.

"It is important to treat people as a ten and tell them as much. Then at times when you need to correct them, correct their behavior. Terms of belittlement are detrimental to the environment that we desire. Mr. Scott asked me what my first thoughts would be if he called me stupid or an idiot."

"And your response was?"

"I recalled our prior manager using such words and how I felt defensive or small. I was less open to bring up any future problems. I told Mr. Scott that it made me apprehensive. He then asked how that affects a relationship with a manager.

"I told him that I had ideas I chose not to bring to my manager because I wanted to avoid possible confrontation. I remember a situation where I had an opinion on a direction to an initiative we were implementing but I chose to say nothing. As it turned out, my opinion would have added value and saved time and money. Eventually we went in that direction. But because of being belittled, that environment stifled me speaking up."

"So how has it improved now?" I asked Mr. Douglas.

"Much improved. As humans we take out our frustrations on each other. That is why it is important that I realize I am a ten. Once I am secure in that, I would not take it to heart if I was belittled and in turn, I do not pass on any belittlement to other employees. Many people put down others because of their own insecurities. The person using belittlement is either passing it on because of their environment or possible lack of self-esteem."

"How do you instill this in others?"

"It starts by simply stating that you're a ten. Mr. Scott announced it to everyone on day one. Then he shows it. He treats everyone with respect. With rewards or consequences, he features rewards, but consequences are not done in a demeaning fashion. Employees respect this and move forward quickly. Mr. Scott tells us, 'Respect your employees today, who may be your customers tomorrow.' I have seen prior managers treat employees as if they were a dime a dozen. Although there is a vast market of potential employees out there, we value our employees and know that each are a ten."

"What results have you seen by this philosophy?"

"We see high morale. Our employees have mutual respect and show it in the quality of their work. They are more open to correction and many times seek it. If they have a problem or feel like they made an error, they are not afraid of speaking up. They are also open to share ideas and opinions because they are not afraid they will be put down. Yet, if their idea or opinions are not incorporated, they respect the decision and move forward."

"What about the statement, 'Your employees today may be your customers tomorrow?' Do you really witness that?"

"Absolutely," he replied. "First, just because someone doesn't work out with us, it does not lower them as individuals. They are a ten. When an employee resigns or we terminate them, there is usually nothing to be embarrassed about. The employee leaves, yet still talks highly of the organization. They refer other potential employees whom they believe will have success in our business. They refer clients or give us leads. Some of our best clients are companies that have some of our prior employees. Think about it, is there no higher accolade than a former employee of yours, who did not succeed, singing your praises? I have also seen some of our former employees become decision makers in other companies, and because of their respect for our environment and staff, they have become good loyal clients."

"Wonderful. Is there anything else that you'd like to add?" I asked.

"Well," Mr. Douglas stated, "this actually plays into the next sign, 'Factual not Negative.'"

"Great, I am all ears," I said.

"Okay," he said, "let's go back to where Mr. Scott had to confront me about the hiring process and my avoidance of him. What I remember most was how Mr. Scott stayed factual. He stated the facts, but he did not speak of me negatively. He defined the facts of my actions and behavior and even the results. By doing this, I didn't become defensive or apprehensive. I actually stayed open-minded, which allowed me to accept responsibility for my actions and behavior. He desires employees to see that even if they disappoint him, that he still values them. Everyone is a ten.

"If you ask yourself, 'What is the desired result as a manager when confronting an employee on a situation that needs addressing or correction?' That result would be for the employee to be open-minded, to listen and understand the facts of the situation clearly. Now while their actions may have been a detriment, this method allows the employee to assume responsibility quickly without embarrassment. Through these stages, the employee is more open for correction. Mr. Scott defines his disappointment. He gives opportunity for response and feedback. By utilizing this method, we as managers clearly define those employees that are coachable and those that are not. Unfortunately, some individuals may not be coachable. So by using the cause-and-effect philosophy, our ultimate result is employees who are coachable, who are more likely to succeed. By using factual not negative, our environment remains positive and respectful."

"Can you give me examples?" I asked.

Mr. Douglas paused for a moment and then stated, "We have many talented sales representatives and each person has their own individual talents which we build from. But there are certain items of information we require all sales representatives to document on the client. This documentation allows management to stay informed on their process, understand the client and the stage, and be able to offer coaching, encouragement, and feedback to the sales representative. We require this information to be documented within our database. Mr. Scott had noticed one sales representative, Terry, consistently not documenting what was required.

"Mr. Scott had Terry pull up several accounts and asked him questions about the clients. Terry knew the answers. Mr. Scott asked why the answers were not in the notes. Terry gave a vague reply and basically stated that he had not had the time to put the notes in the client's records. Mr. Scott told him, 'Terry, I appreciate that you know the information about the clients. However, I am disappointed that the information is not in the account records. Now I ask and I require that you list the information in each client record that you manage. I also need to know that you understand this."

"So what was Terry's response?" I asked.

"Mixed," Mr. Douglas replied. "Mr. Scott obviously laid out his expectations and desires very clearly. He even finished it with a statement defining Terry's understanding and buy-in. But Terry actually questioned Mr. Scott."

My eyebrows went up.

"Terry told Mr. Scott, 'Isn't it enough that I know it? Why is it so important that it be in the clients' notes?'"

"And what was Mr. Scott's reaction?" I asked.

"Mr. Scott very calmly stated, 'Two reasons. The first is for me to ensure that we as a business provide the best service for our clients. With the information I require in the clients' records, I can best help define if we are offering the client the best solutions and also define other concerns. The second reason is it allows my managers or me to help coach you or learn from you. Our job is to help you with your success as well as our client's satisfaction. These notes help me to better assist you.'"

"How did Terry respond?"

"Well," Mr. Douglas said, "He was a little defensive. He had been very successful with us and he asked Mr. Scott, 'Doesn't my success show that? Wouldn't your time be better spent with someone else who needs help?'"

"What was Mr. Scott's response?"

"Mr. Scott's response was quick. He said, 'Terry, if your notes had this information it would help define that for me. My time and energy are very important to me. If your client notes were defined as such, then I could manage that time and energy where needed. First, even I learn daily. You might possibly be of help to me to pass on your success to others. Second, I might wish to reward you with key accounts because of your success, but I cannot unless you adhere to my requirements.'"

"That sounds like a positive response," I said.

"Yeah, I thought so," Mr. Douglas said. "But Terry was still a little defensive. And he told Mr. Scott that he appreciated consideration for key accounts but was busy enough. He then stated he felt he was not in need of help."

"Wow. What happened?"

"Mr. Scott stayed calm. He went right into one of Terry's client records and asked Terry, 'So, what is your next step with this client?' Terry stated what service he was planning to propose. Mr. Scott asked Terry what had assisted him in making his determinations. Terry answered and then Mr. Scott gave him some suggestions on what he would do. Mr. Scott laid out more questions to ask the client that would assist in defining a better solution. Mr. Scott then asked Terry to pick up the phone to call the client."

Mr. Douglas continued, "Terry called the client while Mr. Scott sat with him. Terry asked the questions which then led to more conversation with the client. Mr. Scott even advised Terry of more questions while he was talking to the client. By following Mr. Scott's advice, Terry uncovered more than what he thought he knew about the client. He had been ready to propose a solution that would have been a piece of the client's needs. By working with Mr. Scott, he defined the right solution for the client."

"Wow," I said shaking my head, "so after the conversation, did Mr. Scott say, 'I told you so'?"

"Just the opposite," Mr. Douglas said. "Mr. Scott congratulated Terry by telling him he did a good job. Mr. Scott confirmed what Terry found out from the client. Terry and Mr. Scott defined the right solution. Mr. Scott then coached Terry with recommendations on handling the client and future objectives."

"So how was Terry responding now?"

"Totally different. He was receptive and excited, and he immediately asked Mr. Scott to help with another client."

"Really?" I said. "Did Mr. Scott scold Terry at any time?"

"No. Mr. Scott coached Terry on the next account and complimented Terry for how he handled the client. Mr. Scott told him, 'You're one of my stars and I thank you. I need you to be an example as others look to your success. I want to reward your execution, but you must do it the correct way. Execute what I require, and we will work smarter together, not harder.'"

"What happened then?"

"Well, Terry became more open. Now he is one of our best at execution. He is always seeking coaching from the managers and from Mr. Scott. Before, Terry would never have sought help. I now witness other sales representatives execute better because they witnessed the whole interaction, coaching, and final results. Our credibility as managers and why we ask for certain things have become more established. Terry actually gets more business out of fewer clients. So he is working smarter, not harder."

"Sounds like a win-win situation. Anything else you wish to add?"

"Yes, I learned from witnessing that situation on how to use factual not negative, because Mr. Scott was never negative. This allowed Mr. Scott to demonstrate the method openly. Others witnessed, learned, and gained inspiration. Mr. Scott stays consistent and not only explains himself but also executes the process of what he is trying to explain. Because of our consistency in following Mr. Scott's example, it is easier to discipline and the consequence side is easier to administer."

"Everything works better when expectations are well-defined," I agreed.

"Yes," Mr. Douglas continued. "Consistency with rewards and consequences also matters. Case in point. Mr. Scott noticed recently that Terry had not executed the proper documentation on a client and asked him if there was a reason the client record was incomplete. Terry was not defensive, he simply stated he had not taken the time to enter the information."

"And Mr. Scott's response?" I was curious.

"Mr. Scott calmly expressed his disappointment and he assigned the client to another representative. Terry humbly apologized and affirmed that he would treat the client records as required. The process was that simple. Mr. Scott thanked Terry and assigned the client to another sales representative and then coached that representative on the client and expected execution."

"How was Terry afterward?"

"Very professional. In fact, the very next day Mr. Scott assigned a new account to him to handle."

"He did?" I was surprised. "Why so soon?"

"Simple. Mr. Scott is consistent in what he expects, so that is why he reassigned the account away from Terry. But Terry exhibited correct behavior by showing professionalism. Mr. Scott determined that simple consequences, his confrontation, corrected the behavior and how Terry corrected and handled himself deserved and earned rewarding. Others saw that it is not the end of the world to have consequences, but it is what you learn from the consequences. This showed others that the quicker you correct yourself, you can be right back on the reward side. Once again, Terry was used as a positive example."

"Sounds smart," I said. "It also seems Mr. Scott likes to focus on rewards more. He seems to focus on the positive."

"As much as possible," he said. "This drives the best behavior. I also like how Mr. Scott confronted Terry. Mr. Scott asked him openly on the circumstances and gave him an opportunity to respond. You can generally determine from there what is an excuse from an employee, and what may be a legitimate reason. Mr. Scott teaches us to be bold in what we stand for but careful for what we fall for."

"I like that," I agreed.

Mr. Douglas smiled. "I have another story. This one is about me. Mr. Scott confronted me on an issue in our management meeting. I was assigned to do something the day prior and got sidetracked by other issues I deemed more pressing. I had not seen Mr. Scott in between to discuss or to inform him. So in the meeting Mr. Scott squarely stated, 'I asked you to complete this task yesterday. Did you complete it? If not, can you explain where you are at with it and why the task is not completed?'"

"What was your reply?"

"I told him the truth that I did not have it completed. I explained what stage the task was in and the reasons I had not completed it. I explained what transpired, what I did, and why I made that decision."

"And his response?"

"He apologized to me. He said, 'I apologize that you got side-tracked. I commend you on taking the initiative that you did.' Mr. Scott then said to the other managers, 'I appreciate and encourage each of you to take initiative like Mr. Douglas did. Please make decisions when you must. I will thank you for making a decision and then coach you on the decision you made.' He then openly coached me through my decision which was insightful for us all. The value of his coaching benefited everyone. I was also impressed by Mr. Scott's humility to apologize. Prior managers I've had would never apologize. Mr. Scott apologizes, means it, and then moves forward. He is not afraid to show humility. By doing so, he is appreciated and respected. We know we can trust him."

"Thank you," I said. "That leads to the next sign. 'Trust yet verified.' Please explain."

"No problem," Mr. Douglas said. "That phrase is something that Ronald Reagan said in regards to the arms treaties. Trust isn't blind. Trust is something that is verified. A simple example is me telling my kids to clean their room before we go to the movies. Even when my kids say their room is clean, I check to verify. Sometimes I am not satisfied, or we have different definitions of a clean room. That difference creates an opportunity for me to coach and correct my children."

"How is it used here?"

Mr. Douglas gave a momentary pause, then said, "In the past, we would trust our employees blindly. Sure we had success, but all employees stray a little. Some employees stray and are unaware of it. We had others that were way off our execution, and because we trusted blindly, we were at a difficult stage of correction. We probably lost many good employees because we trusted blindly. So with trust yet verified, we implement systems that we execute as managers to verify continual employee execution. This is a daily management task and initiative. It actually is our main purpose, as it allows us to correct and coach, so everyone learns. Our consistency is important. Our employees now realize that trust yet verified is a benefit. Trust yet verified keeps each employee tuned up and working and executing the most productive way possible."

"I think I understand. Can you give me an example?"

"Sure," he said. "Let's first go back to the example about my kids cleaning their room. My teenage daughter would keep a messy room. I made a rule that if her room was not cleaned by each Friday she would not be allowed to go out on the weekend. The difficulty I encountered was my wife would let our daughter slide and allow her to go out even with a messy room. We were our daughter's superiors but managed her inconsistently. This sent the wrong message. Human nature will take advantage of the circumstance. My daughter knew to ask her mother if

she could go out before I got home. By not having been held accountable, she developed bad habits of laziness and a lack of responsibilities.
Children with a lack of discipline will suffer in society. By not holding
our daughter accountable, we were harming her.

"One Friday I arrived home and our daughter was already out
for the evening and her room was not clean. However, she made the
mistake of coming home with her friends to pick up a few items. I
confronted her and informed her that because her room was not clean
as my rule defines, she was not going to go out that evening. I told her
she had to stay in and that I would take her friends home."

"What did your daughter do?"

"She was embarrassed and thought I was unreasonable for spring-
ing this on her because her mother always let her go out. She promised
to clean her room later. Even though she believed I was unfair, I stood
my ground. I simply asked, 'Did I not state the rule that if your room
was not clean by each Friday that you would not be allowed to go out
on the weekends?' Obviously her answer was yes. So I asked, 'Then
why are you surprised?'"

I nodded. "So what happened?"

"Well," Mr. Douglas replied with a grimace, "the problem was due to
the inconsistency between my wife and me. Our daughter took advantage of the situation, but I see how our daughter suffered because of
the lack of accountability. She had struggles in school and employment
because she developed insecurities from that lack of accountability."

"How do you see this correlate to business?"

Mr. Douglas spoke softly, "If we do not have the systems in place
of trust yet verified, then our employees will develop bad habits. If we
become aware of them in the early stages, it becomes easier to correct. Naturally human nature will also have some employees testing
what they can get away with. Trust-yet-verified systems eliminate the

opportunity for bad habits. In the same manner, our management team must be consistent. If things are done daily, continually, and consistently, it becomes a normal process and is a positive.

"If we do not execute consistently and then attempt to correct and take the big stand, like I did with my daughter, the employee will have the same reaction. The fact that it was a pre-stated rule or condition is irrelevant because by allowing the behavior to continue, you have condoned it. To the employee it is unfair because they have been allowed to get away with their behavior. So consistency is very important. It is imperative to always communicate to all employees trust yet verified and how it correlates to their job performance and success. Nothing should ever be a surprise to any employee."

"Thank you," I said. "Are there any particular things that you have implemented in requirements or processes that you classify as trust yet verified?"

Mr. Douglas answered, "Actually, there is not any one thing that jumps out. It starts with the simple things. By using cause-and-effect philosophy, we as management looked at what were the common causes of employee failure. Then we defined at what stage we could define correct and incorrect behavior. Naturally the ultimate effect wanted is a steady, stable employee. But looking closer, when we use trust yet verified with corrected behavior, we then create a positive teaching effect. So with this in mind, we developed management processes for us to verify important areas for execution. The example I used about Mr. Scott and Terry in regard to client notes was an example of using trust yet verified."

"Is there anything hard about trust yet verified?"

"Yes," he said, "It is too easy to get away from being consistent. First you miss a day, and then two, and then more. It becomes easy to allow yourself to get caught up in other things. Sometimes there are more pressing items that come up, but generally we only fool ourselves. Employees will witness this occurring and even count on your inconsistency. Short term success will even fool you of its importance and then it becomes hard to catch up and even harder to hold employees accountable. Mr. Scott desires us to help hold each other accountable. If things occur we believe are more pressing, we will ask each other for help. I utilize Mr. Scott and he welcomes it. Mr. Scott has no problems with me approaching him and asking straight forward questions on things that may be pressing and seeking his advice on what I should do.

"He coaches me. Sometimes he will tell me to do the pressing item and he will do my follow up. Either way, it creates a positive for me as I grow by Mr. Scotts' coaching and by his involvement. I realize now how we actually do our employees a disservice by not utilizing trust yet verified. Our responsibility to our employees is to provide an environment of success. I have never heard of an employee complaining because of their success."

"Absolutely," I agreed. "Now let's talk about your fourth sign. 'Shortcuts Get You Lost.'

"Sure," Mr. Douglas said. "It correlates closely with trust yet verified. We have systems and requirements in place in each area of our business. Every employee is accountable for execution. Unfortunately, it is part of our human nature to want to take shortcuts. The danger with shortcuts is they sometimes work, which convinces us to continue. But shortcuts will get you lost."

"How so? I asked.

"Shortcuts will have you believe that you will succeed quicker. But eventually a shortcut will lead you astray, causing you to have to back up and redo a process that you left out. Clearly the shortcut got you lost and then cost you more time to correct it. When an individual has early success when taking a shortcut, they are apprehensive to correct their behavior and often do not take the steps to correct it. This will cause that individual to fail. It is imperative by how we manage, using trust yet verified along with rewards or consequences, that we catch the bad behavior of shortcuts early and correct it. We must reward correct behavior. When someone takes a shortcut and has success, it is imperative that we do not reward it. We must immediately correct and coach the individual to change their behavior. The danger in rewarding success from a shortcut is you encourage others to follow in the exact same manner. The individual involved will believe that their action was correct. We must not give legitimacy to the wrong behavior. Our response needs to be the same based on their behavior, not on their result."

Mr. Douglas continued, "Mr. Scott told a story about when he was growing up and was walking home from school. He had a route set by his parents that was obviously safe. Mr. Scott, however, witnessed other kids taking a route through a wooded area. Now although he never saw them exit, he knew that they lived around him, so somehow they succeeded and made it through to the other side. Tempted, and desiring to get home quickly one day for a TV show, young Mr. Scott took the shortcut and ended up lost and became frightened.

"Eventually he was able to make it back to where he entered into the woods. He was back where he started and the attempt of a shortcut had actually cost him time. He of course was able to make it home from there on his set route but his choice made him miss his TV show, plus he also received punishment from his worried mother. The ultimate danger, other than his well-being, was if young Mr. Scott would have found his way through the woods and actually saved time. That result would have given him a false sense of security and convinced him that shortcuts worked. Because of false security, young Mr. Scott might decide to take more shortcuts while traveling, and then find himself really lost. If not caught and corrected early, the lesson will be a harder lesson of failure, and even become harder to change that behavior. This is why we need to catch the behavior of shortcuts and correct the behavior in each employee early on."

"Yes, but isn't it your goal to do things as efficient as possible, with the highest productivity? What differentiates a shortcut from a method that is efficient and productive?" I asked.

"You just answered your own question. A proper method or system or requirement is efficient and productive. A proper method takes cause-and-effect philosophy into account. It considers what is best and what benefits the client, company, and employees. If we provide a service with taking a shortcut, the client ultimately suffers, and eventually so do we as a business. Quick gain is no gain. If we sell services without utilizing our methods to ensure that we are providing the proper solution, we may see a quick gain, but actually we did a disservice to our clients and to our business. Executing things properly can still be expedient but factors in all perspectives."

"Okay," I said, "so what are some characteristics of someone taking shortcuts?"

"Ultimately they chase things. Whether it is in sales, service, operations, or any other department, that individual did not follow the system and requirements, and because of that, did not define things clearly. That individual may also be blind to their circumstance, so they will continue to chase and struggle. My father would always use the expression, 'If you find yourself going around in circles, you probably cut too many corners.' I understand that statement more now than when I was a child.

"When you are chasing or going in circles, it is best to stop cold turkey, reevaluate, reorganize, implement and execute what you cut out by taking a shortcut, and then move forward. It is beneficial for management to define and discover shortcuts, confront them, and correct and coach through them. We must recognize the behavior, call time out, correct the behavior, and implement the execution needed to move forward. On a younger tenured employee, we may walk the individual further down the process so they may start to see the success that their corrections made. This success brings legitimacy to management, as well as our methods, systems, and requirements. By utilizing cause-and-effect philosophy, we are able to evaluate the cause, and then define the ultimate effect we desire, which allows us to correct the situation and the behavior. Obviously we utilize rewards or consequence in each circumstance. The quicker we can reward, the quicker the correction. Remember, a reward can be as simple as a compliment and encouragement."

"So who defines your methods, systems and requirements?"

"We all do," he answered. "We as managers discuss processes along with Mr. Scott. I have also witnessed valuable feedback from our employees. We ask and welcome all opinions. Mr. Scott encourages discussion and then we decide. The decision is explained and communicated fully and then we execute. By allowing employees to be able to speak openly, yet professionally, we gain their buy-in on the final decision and direction, even if they disagree."

"Do some still fight it if they do not agree?"

"Most move forward and execute. From their experience, they respect the process and the decisions. Because of consistency of execution and follow up, they know our expectations. Yet they also know that if any snags occur or unexpected or undesirable results arise from execution, they'll be able to offer their feedback. Mr. Scott knows by humility of openness to feedback that this allows us to tweak our execution a little, or a lot. The focus is more about making it right and effective instead of any, 'I told you so' comments."

"Thank you so much for taking time with me today." I was pleased with our discussion. "What four key points do you think would be most important for me to take away?"

Laughing, Mr. Douglas replied, "Talk about putting me on the spot. Let's see. I would say number one is to first understand and believe that you are a ten. No matter what anyone else may say or do, they cannot take that away from you. Once you understand that about yourself, you will then realize and believe the same about others. Be sure to treat them accordingly. Number two would be to correct behavior factually, not negatively. Correction done any other way draws attention away from what is important, which is correcting the behavior. Number three is to be consistent with trust yet verified. All managers must believe and have buy-in for that consistency. If not, you will get similar results like I had with my daughter due to the inconsistency of my wife and me. Employees will believe in trust yet verified as their success grows.

"Number four, forgo shortcuts. You know I have five basic steps on training all employees. Tell them why, show them how, get them started, keep them going, help them reproduce. If I execute these consistently, I increase their opportunity for success, as well as mine. If I try to take a shortcut, that individual will become lost. Most employers actually cut out number one: tell the person why. Because we consistently explain and communicate, we have developed a better environment of happy, successful employees."

I stood up to shake hands with Mr. Douglas. "Thank you so much. Now I would like to meet with Mr. Charles, the manager of the sales department. Can you direct me?"

"No," he said laughing. "It's time to eat now. Let me buy you lunch in our cafeteria, and then you can meet with Mr. Charles."

CHAPTER THREE

THE MYTH OF COMPLEXITY[3]

Mr. Douglas and I returned from the cafeteria ten minutes before lunch break was over and I was surprised to see many of the sales staff already back at their desks getting organized for the afternoon. I could feel the energy here. Mr. Douglas walked me over to Mr. Charles's cubicle area in the sales department.

Mr. Charles shook my hand as we sat down. His cubicle was actually part of the sales department, not separated. I wondered about privacy of a manager, but I figured I would find out more as we discussed our topics. Mr. Scott briefly interrupted us. It was evident by their conversation that Mr. Scott was going to cover for Mr. Charles while he was pulled away by me.

"Anytime I'm pulled away," Mr. Charles explained, "whether it is for meetings with clients, training, or even for time off, Mr. Scott or our other manager in this department covers for what we do daily. This consistency benefits our sales staff as they know that they are always being supported. That is why it is important that we communicate and for Mr. Scott to know any time that we may be drawn away from our daily tasks. He'd rather not have it as a surprise, as being behind only will hurt our staff. I know I can go to him in confidence to let him know of things I have to do. On some occasions, he actually coaches me on priorities, so this openness has brought new learning situations to me."

Looking around the sales floor, I was impressed by the interaction and activity. I guess I expected a scene like the old movie Wall Street where people would wait for the bell in order to start working. Here people were busy, even as others arrived back from lunch break. By the end of lunch break, everyone was back working. Mr. Scott was active and busy as well as the other manager in the sales department.

Mr. Charles notified his receptionist that he would be in an interview and that Mr. Scott would be available to assist. Mr. Charles was conservatively dressed in a shirt and tie and his coat hung in his cubicle. He was well-groomed and his work area was organized with a lot of files. Once again, I observed several signs in his cubicle area. The first sign read, "Did I give them the benefit of my time?" The second sign read, "You cannot train character." The third sign read, "Confrontation is a benefit." And the fourth read, "Share yourself and your employees."

"Mr. Charles," I said, "I noticed that you have several signs hanging in your cubicle area as did Mr. Douglas and Mr. Scott. Did Mr. Scott recommend posting signs?"

"Mr. Scott inspired me, but he does not require signs," Mr. Charles smiled. "After Mr. Scott took over here, he explained to me that he believes that by visibly posting his beliefs, they help him focus. It is also like wearing your heart on your sleeve. Everyone sees your areas of focus and your beliefs. It was clearly self-accountability for Mr. Scott, as all employees would naturally observe his actions in comparison to his beliefs. I saw it as a motivator for him, but also for our employees, as his actions did correspond with his beliefs and his integrity. We quickly grew to trust him. We see him as genuine and honest.

"I asked Mr. Scott if he thought that it would be a good idea if I did the same thing. He first wanted me to understand why he did it. It was important to him that I realized our employees would judge me according to my actions in correlation to my beliefs on my signs. Mr. Scott emphasized that with posting signs, it would be important that I be humble and realize and admit when I error. I recalled a time when Mr. Scott had slipped up in one of his belief areas and how he had quickly apologized. It was simple, quick, yet genuine. I also remember his openness to critique and know of times when he invited critique or other insights."

I nodded. "Mr. Scott is humble and I am learning in my interviews that he provides a wonderful example for his managers to model," I said.

"Yes," Mr. Charles agreed. "Mr. Scott wanted me to realize that careful thought had to take place before I choose my focus areas for my signs. I asked how he chose his. He said that obviously they must first correlate to me as a person, to my position and my final objectives. He cautioned about playing a game with the method, such as choosing something that is already being executed. I had to understand that my intent would not be to pat myself on the back. He stated that it is okay to pick something being executed, as long as my intent is to further continue its execution, improve it, and be a benefit to others. An important parameter should be, "Would it make me grow and advance as well as our employees and our business?"

"That makes sense," I agreed.

Mr. Charles continued, "I asked Mr. Scott for his critique and help developing my four focus areas. I also asked him what were some of the areas that he had witnessed. This exercise allowed me to come up with my original signs. As we make improvements or new areas of focus come about, I then use the same exercise and get Mr. Scott's feedback to change or add a sign stating that focus."

"Great" I said. "let's start with your first sign which reads, 'Did I give them the benefit of my time?' Can you explain this message and how it applies to your focus?"

"Sure," Mr. Charles replied. "Prior to Mr. Scott taking over, we were more focused on numbers and statistics. We managed by numbers and made our final decisions on employee personnel based on those numbers. Now understand, numbers do have their significance, but we lost the true focus of what established them or the cause. I remember early on in a discussion with Mr. Scott in a staff meeting, the subject was brought up assessing our sales personnel. I mentioned an individual who I classified as someone I believed wasn't going to make it because of his numbers. Mr. Scott asked me what was my plan for this person. I said if his numbers did not improve by the end of the month, I would release him. You see, it was common that we let people go at the end of the month."

"How did Mr. Scott respond?"

"He inquired more, asking what I felt this person's weaknesses were and what areas of improvement did I see that would make that employee successful. I remember thinking Mr. Scott would be impressed because I knew the answers. I could tell him this person's weakness and needed areas of improvement. He then asked about another sales employee who had midlevel success. Once again I could reply on this person's weaknesses and needed areas of improvement.

"Then Mr. Scott asked if his success would improve with attention in that area. I answered, 'Absolutely.' Mr. Scott then asked the same about the first employee who I was considering releasing. If that person were to improve in his needed areas, would he be worth keeping? Again, my answer was yes. Then Mr. Scott asked me to describe what my plan was for both. I was a little confused. Mr. Scott asked me to explain what I did previously with each employee and asked me to not only point out their weaknesses but what I did to coach and train the employee through their weaknesses."

"And your response was?" I asked.

"I felt embarrassed. I realized that although I had mentioned weaknesses on each, I never really coached them on it, yet alone made a plan of training. I admitted as much to Mr. Scott."

"What was his response?"

"He told me my job is more than to identify the employees' weaknesses. I have to give them the benefit of my time. He said, 'Only when you can answer that you've given an employee the benefit of your time and their weaknesses still do not improve can you let them go.'"

"How did you take that?"

"I asked Mr. Scott to clarify and coach me. It opened an area of opportunity for me. He explained that our responsibility is to all employees. As an employer and as a business, we owe it to all employees to hire, train, and maintain the best employees. With that in mind, when someone does not fit that category, we also owe it to all employees to let them go so they can go on with other opportunities. The problem lies when we fail to give them the benefit of our time."

"Did Mr. Scott explain how that is a problem?"

"He pointed out several eye-opening areas. First, that when we don't give someone the benefit of our time, we actually prolong the situation. This is indicative on why our terminations were more at the end of each month. Mr. Scott said we stopped being managers and became monitors. Managers will recognize the areas of weaknesses and get involved with the employee and coach them through it. A coach will be positive, yet disciplined and demanding. A monitor will focus on numbers. As a monitor, we may think we are managing by pointing out numbers or informing the employee the need for improvement and maybe even help point out their weaknesses. But if we do not coach through the process and find the cause to correct the behavior, we have not managed. Monitoring created the environment of end of the month terminations with low morale. Some employees would give up as it became so common. Personally, I don't know how many former employees might have succeeded, but I can think of many that we failed."

I appreciated Mr. Charles's honesty. "Can I ask you a question? Mr. Scott spoke earlier about spending your energy and time with those that warrant it. By giving all employees the benefit of your time, does that not contradict this?"

"Absolutely not!" Mr. Charles said. "It parallels with the process. As you give an employee the benefit of your time, you will quickly recognize who warrants your energy. It singles out quicker those that will not have success. By using this process consistently, terminations are not focused at month end but when recognized and determined by the lack of the employees' behavior modification. After all, this is what drives their results. It allows us to deal with the causes which drives effects."

"So after your coaching, what were some of the results you witnessed?"

"First, it helped me grow. I guess you can say I was receiving the benefit of Mr. Scott's time. I would seek Mr. Scott's council on each employee. Then I would give that employee the benefit of my time. Mr. Scott and I would then assess progress and further strategize. By giving them the benefit of my time and by receiving the benefit of Mr. Scott's time, I benefited. It was easy to recognize those who could change behavior and improve and those who could not. The employees would also recognize it themselves, and it would be no surprise. Before, even if an employee's numbers were not at the level needed, many would believe they could still make it. Now we can point to the behavior and know. We can document the behavior with the employee and derive game plans and strategy. With the documentation, there are no surprises. No one likes turnover, but prolonging turnover is harmful too. Your environment suffers as well as the individual. Managing the cause first, which drives the behaviors, reduces integrity issues that pertain to areas of required numbers."

"What about the employee that gives you every effort on behavior change yet still does not succeed?" I asked. "What do you do to improve them or save them?"

"Mr. Scott always says, 'If you give me every bit of effort, I will give you every bit of my patience and my time.' So certainly we would give them the benefit of our time. But once again, by giving that benefit of time, we quickly recognize the employees' suitability for the job. I think we all have probably seen this type of situation before. I think about myself and the jobs I am not suited for. If I was hired as a construction worker, I might work hard and do everything requested of me, but my abilities would still limit me. Simply stated, that job just is not for me. Sometimes we must come to that conclusion on an individual.

"When I was faced with that circumstance, Mr. Scott helped me see that we actually owe it not only to our employees, but more importantly, to that individual, to release them. The timeliness of our action is important. Prolonging release builds a false sense of comfort to that employee, because as failure continues to present itself, it becomes difficult as a manager and more difficult to the employee to comprehend. Your entire personnel are always involved and may see this as being unfair. Staying consistent, even when difficult, earns credibility and respect. Your employees recognize your fairness. The difficulty as a manager is if the employee is really trying, which you admire and appreciate. But go back to the example of me being a construction worker. How long would I linger on? Could that company execute better with a more qualified employee? Is that company being faithful to all their employees by keeping me? Eventually as I move on, will I accept it as a failure or that I tried and it just did not suit me? The quicker I move forward with another more suitable opportunity, the quicker I can gain success in my life and in employment. This is exactly why we owe it to the employee in question. The employee can leave knowing that their effort was appreciated, and that you value them as an individual. Many of our best clients are former employees who fit this category."

"I would have to agree with you," I said. "I've seen too many times at different jobs where a likable employee would linger in failure simply because he was likable and did give the effort. Then when finally released, other employees would actually feel it was unfair because of sadness that they were there so long."

"That is exactly my point."

"Can you further expand on the results?"

"Sure," Mr. Charles said. "Now as we give an employee the benefit of our time, it allows us time for coaching and more importantly, growth. If termination is a result, it is well defined and timely, not prolonged. End of the month is not feared but enjoyed. Terminations are now timely and focused on cause or behavior with effects being tangible. The results are our terminations happen when the decision is made, not just at the end of the month."

"If someone's numbers or requirements lack, but good behavior is there, would you possibly keep them?" I wondered.

"If we determine their behavior is bringing about improvement, yes."

"So what other benefits are derived by giving someone the benefit of your time?" I asked.

"Naturally by being involved, I am able to coach, encourage, and correct. It is important that when we fix a problem, and as some may still occur, that we are able to recognize potential problem areas and correct them prior to their becoming a problem. By being involved, we set high expectations, but our involvement manages to expectations instead of monitoring them. By giving the benefit of my time, I'm able to recognize certain areas of needed improvement and we focus with our staff to improve it."

"Can you name some of those areas?"

"Sure, I'll name a couple. The first one would be the area of shortcuts, which we coach to eliminate. By being involved, we are able to recognize the symptoms and correct behavior. We do teach a patient aggressiveness."

"What is a patient aggressiveness?"

"Simple. Obviously the goal is the desired result. We teach and coach our employees to be aggressive, to move the process forward, but with patience. Without that patience, shortcuts occur. By giving the benefit of my time, I can recognize the difference. Then the other example would be a common problem in any job, employees putting things off until tomorrow."

"But sometimes isn't that necessary?"

"Sure, but my involvement can help determine that and help them prioritize. Our employees benefit when they are the most effective. Putting things off can hinder that and alter their priorities. My father used to tell me, 'Our future would be assured if we did as much today as we plan tomorrow.' Think about it. Human nature teaches us tomorrow we can do a lot. Why not do today what we can, making us more effective tomorrow?"

"I would agree with that," laughing as I spoke. "Do you have anything else to share on this topic?"

"Just that it is imperative for a healthy environment for all employees. I am at peace with my decisions when I now ask, 'Did I give them the benefit of my time?' If for any reason I am not sure, I make sure I do."

"Thanks," I said. "Your next sign reads, 'You Cannot Train Character.' It seems pretty much a statement. Can you expand on it?"

"It is a statement, and also a constant daily reminder. We make a mistake when we believe that we can train or change character, or we remove it from our equation of employees we maintain."

"How is that? Please explain more."

"Certainly," Mr. Charles said. "First let's briefly define character. There are many meanings that can fall under the umbrella of character. Honesty, integrity, morals, values, unselfishness, and the simple facts of what is right and what is wrong. Character is also how one carries themselves in regard to morals and concern for others, as well as for the company. Obviously we probably can define more, but I'll utilize another word used in a business environment in regard to an employee with lack of character, and that is a cancer."

"A cancer?" I asked.

"Yes, a cancer," he replied. "The term cancer is used as it parallels what a cancer does in the human body. Cancer is bad and unhealthy and if it goes untreated, it infects other parts of the body. Well, an employee deemed as a cancer that goes untreated will infect other employees."

"I understand the comparison. So with an employee being a cancer, how do you treat it?"

"Good question. Unlike human cancer, once we define a cancer, we opt to cut it out. Experience shows this is proven to be the best option. A cancer will give you visible signs to define, confront, coach, and document before the surgery. The problem lies when you believe you can medicate the cancer."

"How is that so? Can't you shrink the cancer in a manner of speaking? Are there not ways to bring about change?"

"You are asking valid questions. The best way for me to answer is for me to take you through some experiences. Then we can talk about each one and possibly answer more questions.

Let's start when Mr. Scott first took over our location. He was big on coaching and training and emphasized concern on employee turnover. We managers wanted to make an impact with our personnel. Well, I had a sales representative, Barney, that had been employed for approximately six months. Barney would be above the minimal requirements each month, so based on our method of termination, he met the statistics and was not a candidate for termination. The problem was because we managed by those numbers alone, we blinded ourselves to his bad character. Barney was above the minimal requirements, but just above them. He was not showing the kind of growth expected or desired for someone of that tenure."

"So what was the problem?"

"Barney was not executing what we were asking. We managers would accept his lip service, when in actuality our counseling never materialized results or behavior change. Because Barney made the minimal requirements, he stayed and we allowed the other employees to witness a bad example."

"How is that so?" I asked.

"We weren't using rewards or consequences, or we were only using it on required numbers, not behavior. Barney did not execute, yet maintained employment. Other employees witnessed this and believed it was okay. This was at least the message we were sending. Mr. Scott confronted me on the situation and I told him, 'I believe this employee will come around.' He then asked if I had given Barney the benefit of my time, and I answered yes, but that I would give more. Mr. Scott allowed me two more weeks."

"I take it Barney failed to change."

"You're correct. I failed to see that I had given him the benefit of my time, and that he failed to change his behavior. I tried to aid his attitude, but Barney was set in his ways. Well, over that two-week period, each day Mr. Scott would coach me. I was amazed with how many opportunities that were presented for me to coach, confront, and attempt behavior change with Barney. It also allowed me to document the instances, and it opened my eyes that he was not going to change. The exercise was good as it allowed me to manage with rewards and consequence and exhibited this to other employees. I'm appreciative of the patience Mr. Scott showed in coaching me through it. Obviously he pretty much knew from the beginning what the final result would be, but teaching me this lesson was also important to him."

"So you let Barney go?"

"Yes, and then Mr. Scott asked me what I learned."

"What did you learn?" I asked.

"First, the obvious, that it is no fun letting people go, but that we owe it to all employees if someone is not a fit, even if they are making minimal number requirements statistically. Second, character needs to be a more important requirement than stats. Mr. Scott pointed out the extra energy I wasted after I had given Barney the benefit of my time. I did not realize I was taking away from other employees who exhibit the character we desire, or even a new hire that we prevented ourselves from hiring as long as we kept this employee."

"How do employee turnover concerns come into this equation?"

"Obviously it is a concern. Mr. Scott pointed out that keeping such a person around can add to turnover if poor habits and lack of change spreads through other employees. He helped me realize that fairness to all employees in regards to character expectation, despite other requirements like numbers, is very important."

"So now would you let go of others that may be showing statistical success?"

"Absolutely, but let's get back to that. Mr. Scott told me about an occurrence that happened early in his management career. In his early twenties, he was a manager in the restaurant fast food business. He had three employees who were of bad character. Mr. Scott said their character flaw was discontent."

"What do you mean, discontent?"

"They would gossip and stir things up. They'd create problems and mask it in other ways such as saying they were simply pointing out problems. Mr. Scott said he tried to satisfy these three and even tried befriending them. He tried different tactics and spent a lot of energy trying to turn them around. Eventually he said that he was the one terminated and sure enough these three employees were a part of the cause. Also the extra attention and energy Mr. Scott utilized on them took away from other areas that hindered his overall performance. Had he eliminated the cancer once he made this determination, he probably would have succeeded. He found out that the three did not last long under the new, more experienced manager. Mr. Scott explained to me that this was a valuable lesson for him."

"That is a good example, but you mentioned letting people go who might be showing some success. Can you give an example of that?"

"Sure, I will give you a couple of examples. Once we had a sales representative that executed well and earned good status. Other sales representatives looked up to Albert. Over time Albert developed habits that had him taking shortcuts. Now understand, we're open to new ideas, but Albert really changed in attitude. This decline showed in how he handled accounts and the lack of his timeliness to be at work or in returning from lunch break. Each of the sales management team would confront the issues and use rewards or consequence, but change would not occur. Albert's sales were declining but still respectable. The problem was our new sales representatives, along with current ones, would look at Albert as a successful one and emulate him. After addressing it continually, and along with Mr. Scott's involvement, we delivered the rehire technique to Albert. Although he committed verbally to change, his actions were the opposite. So, Mr. Scott made the determination and released him."

"I bet that sent a strong message."

"Actually, our sales staff reacted with shock. The office talk was that they could not believe we made that determination, and they didn't understand the decision."

"Why was that?"

"We had allowed the situation to linger, and Albert was an employee of presumed status or position. Employees had become accustomed to the situation and his perceived success. People can believe an element of unfairness is involved when you make the termination decision, because of the behavior occurring over a prolonged period."

"Well, I'm sure that went away in time?"

"This is where Mr. Scott did something that really impressed me."

"What was that?"

"He called the entire sales staff together and addressed it. He did it as a means to refocus everyone quickly, with eliminating gossip. How he did it earned credibility with everyone."

"How is that?"

"Well, understanding that there is potential liability in everything we do or say, Mr. Scott told a story. He talked about a football team he followed, who had a Pro Bowl center for years. This center was elite and a leader. But as time went on, there would be stories in the newspaper of this player missing practice or a team meeting. Surprisingly one day this player was released. The other players were surprised. This guy was a Pro Bowl player, which means that he was at the top of his game. When the coach addressed the team, the coach simply stated that there are certain things required of all, as well as some special benefits that veterans may earn. But when it came down to the fundamentals of what is required, the coach believed that he owed it to the rest of his players out of respect to make the change. The coach emphasized the importance to the fundamentals and his values and principles. Therefore, he determined that the change was needed."

"Wow, did it hurt the team's performance that year?"

"Funny thing, that team won the Super Bowl that year. The rookie replacement for that player ended up a Pro Bowler with a long career. The coach hadn't realized how much that player's attitude affected his entire team. Someone who is a cancer shows selfishness, which hurts a team. Now I'm not saying that when you let go a good player for these reasons you'll win the Super Bowl, but I am hard pressed to think of an instance where performance did not improve."

"Great. What about your other story?"

"Well, my other story is another good example because this person was very talented. I mention this example because it brings out the dangers in people that are cancers with talent. We will blind ourselves to their bad character, believing we can manage around that or we convince ourselves that their talents are worth it. We fail to realize the harm they'll do. Sometimes we would even rehire these people back, hoping they have changed or believing we can change them. This is a true example of 'You can't train character,' and when you keep it on that level, your decisions are easy."

"Okay, now that you've prepped me, give me the details."

"Well, this person was my previous manager."

"Wow, okay, so the details?"

"My previous manager was a highly talented individual, articulate, intelligent, and a very good teacher. Zeke had many natural gifts and talents that parallel our business. Being a sales oriented organization, he understood the sales process that benefited our clients and business and was very good at breaking it down into training tidbits for our employees. Many times I was in awe of him."

"As you describe him, I fail to identify any flaw; surely these talents were an asset?"

"Absolutely," Mr. Charles said. "Obviously, to obtain the position within our corporation, Zeke must have exhibited a potential ability for success, and these talents correlated to that potential."

"So where did he go wrong?"

"Zeke lacked character. His flaws were the ones I described previously of a person of discontent. As our manager, he openly griped about his superiors and our company. He would verbalize to us his opinions on company decision or direction he deemed poor. Another flaw of his character was ego and pride. Ego and pride may be a benefit at times, but not when it takes the form of selfishness."

"Can you explain that further?"

"Sure. As our manager, his ego had him always taking the credit. When things were good, it was about him. But on the other side, he never took the blame. It seemed we were to blame on issues that were not right. This is where morale really started to suffer. But there were hidden dangers also.

"Because of Zeke's talent for coaching sales techniques, he could awe and earn respect in that area. As an employee, you knew he had much to teach you, so you'd mask your personal feelings of his bad character because you still had the benefit of learning. Yet his behaviors of not taking blame, and blaming others for things he also had responsibility in, would create employees' unfavorable opinions of him. Zeke didn't show respect to others, but demanded it for himself. As time went by, people would blind themselves to their true feelings about his character because of his gift of coaching sales. But activating events, occurring daily, but on different levels, would bring out his bad character behaviors and make an uncomfortable and unpleasant environment. Employees would welcome the positive and survive through the negative. Eventually you force yourself to become blind to the atmosphere and others will also."

"How does it get resolved?"

"First, you must maintain your good character traits and not be influenced by the person with bad character. Second, you must trust that those above this person recognize the situation and value good character above talent. When asked about the situation, I recommend communicating as honestly as possible. Remember, it is your character test."

"Any concern that it will make you look bad, or what about retaliation?"

"Absolutely there may be some fear on both, but then that is why it is important to exhibit the proper character always. Follow the adage: 'Do the right thing even when nobody's looking.' I heard this once from Thomas Henderson, the former Dallas Cowboy who himself struggled, went to prison, and then turned himself around and now helps youth programs and believes that doing the right thing when nobody is looking is the true test of character. I truly believe proper character gets noticed. The next advice is to be professional. Unlike my manager's character, I did not complain about him in front of employees, but I did address him openly. There came a point I realized the ineffectiveness of not confronting my boss due to his nature. When asked by any superior, I would respond honestly, yet professionally. It came to a point where I had to determine based on my values whether to stay employed here or choose to leave. I had to weigh both options."

"So you decided to stay?"

"Yes. I valued our employees and our business. I maintained my integrity and made sure I did not become a cancer myself."

"What happened?"

"Zeke was let go."

"That must have relieved everyone."

"Actually it brought mixed reviews. This is the danger of a cancer that is talented. Many admired his talents and benefited from them.

To them, the talents far outweighed his character. Many actually questioned the move of him being let go."

"What happened next?"

"Fortunately Mr. Scott came in. We quickly felt the low morale burden lifted. Many didn't even realize they had this burden until their morale increased. Mr. Scott was humble, motivating, and accessible. Although Mr. Scott may have lacked some of Zeke's knowledge, he acknowledged it and found answers. It really brought a sense of team and family here."

"Any drawbacks?"

"The drawbacks were the length of time that the cancer of our manager was allowed to grow. A cancerous person not only affects you, it infects you. Remember, a cancerous employee is someone you determined won't change. Once you determine a cancer, you must cut it out. Delaying it only causes harm and allows it to spread. So when hiring, training, and in continued employment, you must put character first. A person with talent and character is great, but a person with talent and a lack of good character is dangerous. Skills, I can train. Character, I cannot."

"Okay, earlier you mentioned about medicated cancer. What did you mean by that?"

"People medicate cancers in many different ways. With my former boss, I tried to avoid the situations that would bring forward cancerous outbreaks. Sometimes I felt like I was walking on eggshells. With an employee I would convince myself I could change them. I would blind myself to their lack of behavior change and functions. Another example is a situation similar to one at my brother's workplace. My brother is a manager of sales for a company where his counterpart is a cancer. This person lacks the people skills to manage and doesn't like change unless he implements it. My brother says that when they have an idea for a change, they make that manager believe it was his idea."

"What dangers do you see in that?"

"I see many dangers. First, you're medicating the situation as best as possible, but a cancer will always spread. You may be trying to believe that you can use the person's talent and medicate the cancer. Second, you're burning valuable energy that is taking away from other valuable areas. Third, you're prolonging the situation and hurting yourself and all others concerned. In all the time you have medicated the situation, you could have replaced the cancerous person therefore working toward the ultimate environment. If your goal is to have the best morale possible, then why delay? It only hurts to delay."

"Good point," I said. "Now let me ask you about your third sign, 'Confrontation is a benefit.' Explain to me this philosophy."

Mr. Charles replied, "First let's define what confrontation is. Many people believe confrontation is an argument or when two opposing beliefs, principles, or circumstance meet and therefore it escalates."

"You're right," I said. "When I first read that sign, I thought it was indicating that arguments were good. I envisioned people arguing, and I could not understand how that could be a benefit."

"Confrontation," Mr. Charles stated, "is when anything detrimental to progress and success as a whole or individual is determined and needs to be corrected. The confrontation is standing face to face with that situation. That situation may indeed be opposing beliefs, principles, or circumstance. Remember your employee's success is your success. With this in mind, Mr. Scott has developed us to be as proactive as possible in our confrontation, just like a good sports coach.

"For example, a good football coach is confronting his players throughout the whole game. When the running back comes out for a play or with the offense, the coaching staff goes over how they are doing in the game. They are confronting the line men on their blocking and making corrections. They are confronting the running back on following their blockers. They are proactively confronting each situation. Now if they ran their football team like many organizations run their business, they wouldn't confront until after the game was over. They would read the statistics and tell the running back to gain more yards next time. By being proactive, they actually get down to details. The more you create the opportunity to coach and confront, the more opportunity for success you'll have. This is how we instill it in our business."

"Confronting is actually opportunities to coach?"

"In most circumstances, yes. When you are coaching immediately on areas that need addressing, you are really confronting an opportunity. First understand the coach is confronting while the game is going on. But in business, much like life, there are many things we put to the side, hoping we don't have to address them. It would be like a football coach ignoring the fact his kicker cannot make a field goal, so he hopes they always score touchdowns."

"What would be wrong if they scored touchdowns instead of field goals?"

"Actually nothing, if that was the result. But the problem is by not confronting the issue, he and the rest of the coaching staff start coaching differently. The result is they become less effective. Turn this situation to a business and you have a company that gradually becomes less effective."

"So how do you confront it?"

"Simple. You address the issue. Understand that by confronting the issue, it does not mean the issue is solved immediately. The confrontation is the start. From there, planning and implementation can take place to start the process to resolution. But remember, you cannot overcome what you do not confront. The quicker you confront each situation, the quicker the resolution. I must also emphasize that your skills as a manager also grow. Watching Mr. Scott, I see him as the most confrontational manager there is. From watching him, I see his people skills, management skills, and the respect that he commands because of it."

"Can you give me some examples?"

"Sure. One way Mr. Scott welcomes confrontation is by having an open door policy. All employees are welcome to come to him with any situation. This allows Mr. Scott to help confront the situation and help that employee overcome it. Mr. Scott is extremely helpful and professional, so it makes employees feel comfortable and not apprehensive. This further opens the door for any future situations. As the employee obtains results, they welcome the confrontation. Now if Mr. Scott needs to address any managers due to these situations brought to him, he uses this confrontation as a means to coach us. That is the basis of his confrontation as it equates then to his coaching. Mr. Scott exhibits an even temperament, even in times of disappointment. He is well respected for this."

"How do managers like this open door policy?"

"I welcome it. At first, we were probably apprehensive. I believe that is because our old manager believed in the chain of command. Please understand, Mr. Scott respects that chain of command also. Mr. Scott's first questions to an employee are to inquire what their manager's thoughts were. But he wants all employees to feel welcome if they are not getting results, need additional help, or if he is the quickest available solution."

"What about the chain of command where Mr. Scott is concerned?"

"Good question. Mr. Scott publicly communicated his belief and practice for that open door policy to work in regard to him also. In fact, when his superiors visit, he makes it a point to enhance our openness and comfort level to them. I once mentioned something to Mr. Scott's superior about a situation we were facing and when he asked for my opinion, I gave my point of view the best I could. My opinion wasn't in complete agreement with Mr. Scott's. Later, Mr. Scott thanked me. Together we confronted that situation and utilized a lot of my opinion. I actually grew from the experience."

"So Mr. Scott wasn't apprehensive about you speaking up or worried that you would embarrass him?"

"No, not at all," Mr. Charles said. "He explained he wants us to grow. He believes that to not have an open door policy would eventually stifle our creativity and communication. As time goes on I see how he humbles himself for our betterment. Mr. Scott points out, as we grow, he grows. The more we find confrontation or coaching opportunities, the more we will grow."

"Agreed. Any other examples?"

"Sure. The next example was on the day Mr. Scott arrived. He addressed all employees and explained his open door policy. He emphasized his openness to be involved. On that first day, one of our sales representatives had something go wrong with our service department servicing their client. Mr. Scott inquired of the details then called the client immediately for that sales representative. He introduced himself and informed the client of the situation. He told them he believes that in business if something does not go correctly it is important to address it immediately. The client was receptive.

"By Mr. Scott addressing the situation immediately, he was able to keep that client's confidence. With Mr. Scott confronting the issue head on, he allowed for a quick solution. He and the client agreed on a resolution and laid the groundwork. All our sales representatives were blown away. Mr. Scott earned immediate respect and credibility. Now understand, before this, most of us managers just wouldn't confront this kind of situation like this. In fact, we would probably hide from it. Sure, we would coach and inform the sales representative of what to do, but we'd leave it in their hands. I remember thinking after Mr. Scott's confrontation how our previous actions only taught our sales representatives to do the same. Why should I get angry if they avoided the client like I did? Mr. Scott's example taught us to confront the client. It was a valuable lesson."

"Wow, I'm sure it was. Did Mr. Scott ask why you didn't call the client?"

"No. It was obvious we were not accustomed to confronting situations like this. Mr. Scott let his actions teach us. After that, I was surprised that several of our sales representatives had issues or needs with clients, which management was unaware of. They seemed to come out of the woodwork. You see, because we didn't confront, we actually taught our employees to bury issues. Quickly each of us jumped on board confronting issues like these. Mr. Scott was open to helping us managers and would coach us as we grew. Now these kinds of issues are confronted by us immediately. This allows us to be more confrontational with positive client issues."

"How is that?"

"Because we address these confrontational situations immediately, this keeps them off our plate. We seek and openly welcome involvement in the positive aspects of partnership building with clients. Every day we managers assist one of our sales representatives in calling a client on positive issues about their business. How can we assist them as a partner? They are extremely receptive. Clients appreciate hearing from management other than times of problems. It assures them of their importance and to witness that we truly feel that way."

"Excellent. Anything else?"

"Another example that I was not directly involved in, but I witnessed, is a delicate issue as it was a pay issue. Our business has grown, and changed greatly over the years. Years ago that change was slower, which had a different effect. Well, we had an issue with how the people on our service side were being paid. A pay system was developed early on when the market for what we do was much different, so it was designed to that format. With the change in the market, the old system did not work with the faster changing market place. The result was unbalanced overpayment on salaries for what our business could absorb, and what market value was. But understand, you're dealing with peoples' pay. To anyone, this is a delicate issue. Mr. Scott worked on a solution. He formatted what truly correlated to the business in terms of today's environment. But now Mr. Scott had to address the situation.

"Mr. Scott confronted the service employees. He also worked with some of their leaders or more tenured employees with their concerns and ideas. Mr. Scott was genuine. He showed the problem and explained how the past process doesn't match the current market. He made a statement that made sense. He asked everyone that if at any time that he would come out with a policy that seemed good on the surface, but over time it was unfair, wouldn't they want and expect him to see the unfairness and change it?"

"And their answer?"

"Everyone said yes. So Mr. Scott simply said, 'Why can't I expect the same of you?'"

"How did they react?"

"They understood. Mr. Scott showed them how the old way didn't work and hurt the business as a whole. He explained our responsibility is for all employees and it was important for him to run a business responsible to all employees. By Mr. Scott confronting the issue, he came across professional and genuine. This allowed for a smoother transition with no hidden resentment. It seems because of confrontation we have drawn closer as a business. There is more trust and respect.

"I remember I once commented on how thankful I was how Mr. Scott confronts everything. He shared a quote I had heard before, 'A real leader faces the music when he doesn't like the tune.'"

"Yes, it may seem easier to ignore situations. Some may believe this is healthy as you stay focused on the positive. What are your thoughts?" I asked.

Mr. Charles replied, "Confronting them is focusing on the positive. There are hidden obstacles that sometimes will reveal themselves. Mr. Scott has taught us that confrontation is such a positive because of the end result. The result is what we focus on. I earlier mentioned my brother. He recently told me his manager now realizes what a benefit my brother is as he makes him confront things he ignored. At first it probably bothered him until he started seeing results. Even while we ignore problems, we still know they are there. That manager is not only seeing the result of overcoming the situation but has one less thing on his mind. He also is seeing the results in the motivation of his employees. Truly, confrontation is a benefit."

"Truly it is. Now your fourth sign reads, 'Share Yourself and Know Your Employee's Dreams.' Can you now explain this?"

"Absolutely. Simply put, we put an emphasis to be personable. This was new to me. With my prior boss and even prior jobs, managers were not personable. They were there to do their job, as were the employees, but we really didn't know each other."

"What do you mean, be personable?"

"First, let me say that being personable does not take away from being professional. I think that is where many get it wrong. To me that is simply arrogance and pride. Mr. Scott led by example. At first I'd see him being visible prior to work hours or after, not only helping employees but also being personable. He would engage employees on their families, dreams and desires, and even share his. I witnessed him talking about sports with employees who like sports. I've seen him talk about his family or vacation trips that he has been on. More importantly is how the employees opened up on their family, goals, desires, etc. The only thing I have not seen Mr. Scott talk about is politics."

"Why not?"

"I asked him that once and Mr. Scott said some topics may cause distractions. People have strong beliefs in politics and a discussion can cause an argument and even bitter feelings. Mr. Scott's goal is to get to know the employee and to represent himself in the human light. This really opens up the employees to him and earns a sense of trust and family. Think about it. In your family, you at times have to face difficult decisions. In our employment family, we do also. Because of the realness and trust, when those times come they are accepted easier and respected. Just like your children may not like to get disciplined, but they eventually realize and see it's out of love and a desire for their greater good. It is very much the same here. I've seen Mr. Scott purposely incorporate themes for the week or for the month that allows us to know each other better."

"Tell me more."

"Certainly. Once Mr. Scott started out the month on 'Who's your hero?' theme. Mr. Scott explained his childhood hero was Carl Yastrzemski, the baseball player. He listed why and wrote down three qualities of that hero. He had each employee do the same. Each employee hung up their listing of their hero at their work area for all to see and share. Mr. Scott advised to try to exhibit the qualities of their hero, and as they do, they actually become their hero. This was motivating and eye opening, as some employees' heroes were surprising and told us a lot about the person we had not realized. As we worked with the employees on a daily basis, we'd talk about their heroes. Many people became more open."

"What about religion? Wouldn't that be in the same category as politics?"

"It can be. Anything that could make someone feel uncomfortable is improper. I visibly see Mr. Scott is a man of deep faith. You can tell by how someone carries themselves. Mr. Scott makes no secret that he does Bible studies, etc., but he doesn't put those convictions on anyone else. The focus of "share yourself" is, I believe, one of the reasons that even former employees still think highly of this business, even if they were not successful here. It is beneficial to be personable."

"What are some things that you talk about with employees?"

"Most people value and cherish their families. I see people light up when talking about their children or asking about their children's interests and their interests. I have found it beneficial sharing mine. When I first experienced this with Mr. Scott, I felt comfortable and more at ease. Coming to work was pleasant and even exciting. I truly see people listen and respect more. Mr. Scott once said something that is so true. "People don't care what you know until they know that you care." This hits home as you witness it. We have a volunteer group we organized to help in our community. Our group decides on issues to help with and amazingly almost all employees participate. That is the measure of our unity."

"I was raised in the business world where personal associations, even in the terms you speak of, were taboo. Does it not cross any line of professionalism?"

"Not in the terms I discussed. True, anything that would make anyone uncomfortable must not be discussed or done. But conversations on peoples' dreams and aspirations are valuable and build that sense of team and family. Most managers that dislike and discourage associating in this manner are just arrogant. They place themselves above their employees. They are in a position above employees but not as a person. This is what Mr. Scott exemplifies. There is a difference from being genuine to being a phony. Employers and managers that do not know their employees' dreams are that much more ineffective."

"Do you have any more instances to add?"

"I could name a hundred examples, but let me tell you about two more. We had an employee whose house was badly damaged during last year's bad storms. Mr. Scott called an all- employee meeting to announce a voluntary collection to help assist this employee. Mr. Scott started the collection that night with a check from himself and one from the company. Over the next few days, we collected money for this employee in her time of need. This was genuine and caring. It was a true example of our unity. This is why even through hard times or difficult decisions, Mr. Scott is trusted. He's genuine. Another instance was when we adopted a needy family around the holidays with gifts, food, and love. To see the joy in giving by our employees just brings a sense of family. Now I know this isn't speaking about their dreams, but it is helping to make some for others. The true benefit was the unity this created. I thrive on this environment."

"Thank you. Let me shift gears. We discussed managing behavior, as well as creating behavior by managing environment. Is this not difficult to incorporate?"

"Actually that's the myth."

"The myth?"

"Yes, the myth of complexity.[4] We believe that it's complex so we don't execute. Reality is our jobs become complex when we don't execute. The key to managing behavior and the environment conducive to creating good results is consistency and execution. If you're inconsistent, you'll send a confusing message. If you're consistent, you must be complete in your execution. Stay on top of these two keys and success will manifest itself. Fail to execute or fail to be consistent and you will be chasing your tail. I have found that consistency and execution create a thriving enjoyable environment. This environment breeds on itself."

"I truly see your point. Before we end our conversation, what four key points would you like me to take away?"

"Four things," Mr. Charles paused. "Number one would be to never underestimate the environment you create and your personal affect and involvement in relation to that environment. This is why each element of consistency is important. We must remember that there is a price to pay for success. Commitment is the price. I must be committed to execution on each facet of what relates to me. This starts from knowing I gave each employee the benefit of my time through everything else that affects our environment. Once again, we must be mindful of cause and effect.

"Number two, realize and remember that a cancerous attitude is no respecter of talent. A cancerous attitude is a cancerous attitude and needs to be diagnosed and cut out. Skills are trainable. Character is not trainable. Once we realize that, we save time, energy, and our culture. Remember a cancerous person not only affects everyone but also infects everyone. It's a danger to your culture. Don't be blinded by someone's skills.

"Three, remember as mountain climbers know, the view is spectacular on the mountain top but life is lived in the valleys. This is why confrontation is a key. Confronting conquers and allows you to climb those mountains. Confrontation is not defined as an argument. Confrontation brings things to an impasse and a point of decision and conquest. Done professionally, it is coaching at its best. It's motivating to your environment. It breeds success.

"Fourth, believe that it is not unprofessional to know your employees' dreams. It's beneficial. Anything tangible to their success creates an environment of unity. You know I realize I'm being watched daily.

How I coach and manage is how our employees grow and succeed. I realize that as I model, our employees grow and succeed. I realize that as I lead, our employees imitate. As I explain, they experiment. As I coach, they apply. As I support, they demonstrate. So as I commission them, they represent. My execution, consistency, genuine quality, professionalism, openness, responsiveness, and motivation are directly tied to their success. That is a responsibility not taken lightly. But it is a responsibility I truly enjoy."

"Mr. Charles, thank you very much. I see why you are successful, and I wish you all the best. I would now like to talk with Mr. Anthony."

"Of course," he replied. "Let me walk you over to his office."

CHAPTER FOUR

KNOWLEDGE IS THE VEHICLE FOR CHANGE

Mr. Anthony was neatly attired in dress slacks, dress shirt, and a tie. His far office wall caught my attention.

The whole wall was decorated as a baseball diamond. It was done in a neat fashion, yet had a childlike feel, similar to an elementary school project. The turf for the outfield and infield was green construction paper. White yarn was used for the first base and third base lines, and also showed the paths from first base to second, and second to third. The pitcher's mound was an oval of brown construction paper. There were young players in each position. The grandstand area showed happy faces cut out of a child's magazine to symbolize fans. There was a fan with a wave like the ocean to symbolize that they were doing the wave. The bases were 12 x 12 squares of white construction paper. Next to each base was a neatly printed message. Home plate read, "Values and Principles." First base said, "Anger and Danger." Second base stated "Problems and Opportunities." And third base, "Knowledge and Change."

Underneath the diamond, below home plate, these words were followed by their definitions. *Values. Principle. Anger. Danger.* Three more words and definitions were listed under *Anger* and *Danger*: *Meek*, *Humble*, and *Temperament*. The words for second base were *Problem* and *Opportunity*, and under them, *Failure* and *Success*. For third base, *Knowledge* and *Change*.[5] My interest was certainly piqued.

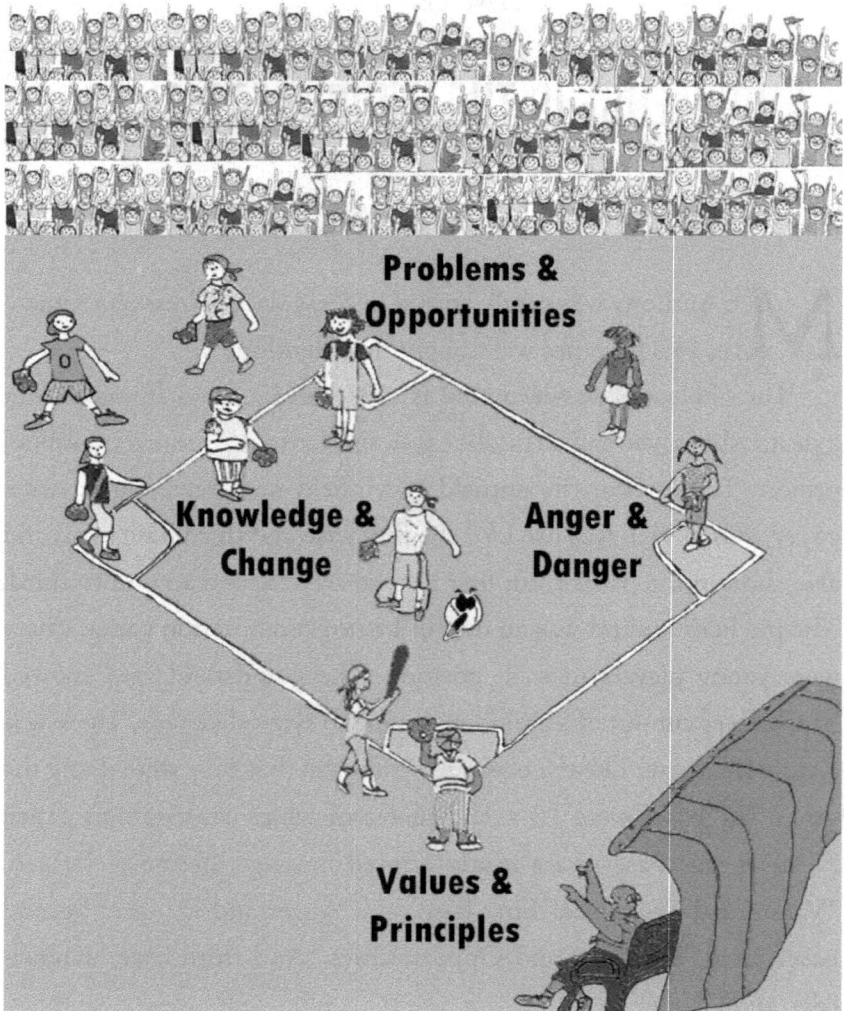

Problems & Opportunities

Knowledge & Change

Anger & Danger

Values & Principles

> Values = a relative or assigned worth or importance; a principle; standard; or quality considered worthwhile or desirable

> Principles = a fixed or predetermined policy or mode of action; moral or ethical standards or judgements collectively

> Anger = a feeling of extreme displeasure; hostility; indignation; or exasperation toward someone or something; rages; wrath; ire

> Danger = exposure or vulnerability to harm or risk

   • Meek = showing patience and humility; gentle

   • Humble = modesty in behavior

   • Temperament = the manner of thinking, behaving, or reacting characteristic of a specific individual

> Problems = a question or situation that presents uncertainty, perplexity, or difficulty

> Opportunities = a chance for progress or advancement

   • Failure = the condition or fact of not achieving the desired end or ends

   • Success = the achievement of something desired, planned or attempted

> Knowledge = understanding gained through experience or study

> Change = to transform [6]

"I appreciate your time," I said. "My day has been eye opening. I am surprised by the openness of everyone. I'm actually impressed with it."

"Glad to hear it," Mr. Anthony stated. "We have a good team here. I believe part of our success is our openness and eagerness to share and learn. I'm sure through our conversations we also learn from you. A third eye view can sometimes see things that we become blind or accustomed to. Remember, we see our culture every day. You're seeing it from an outside perspective. That perspective is valuable to us."

"I guess I never saw it that way. I had thought perhaps you would be protective."

"I could see where you may think that. But what we do here is pretty simplistic. It is no big secret. Our execution of what we do is why we have success. The old line about 90% execution is true."

"What makes your execution better?" I asked.

"I would say it comes down to how we treat our employees. Mr. Scott brought in a people skills environment that places our focus on our people. Those skills develop good behaviors and a healthy environment."

"Environment is more important than quick results or immediate success?"

"I would simplify that by saying any success, whether immediate or developed over time, will not survive unless the right environment is developed," Mr. Anthony said. "There are many successful environments. I've seen successful autocratic managers, but I believe our environment will outlive that autocratic environment. It's more long-term. If other factors play into one's success, like the economy, our environment stands a better chance, as each employee has a sense of ownership and team. If you look at history, you'll see it. When economies suffer, many businesses suffer also. Yet in each industry, there are strong survivors. There are businesses that still show profits while others in the industry do not. You recently saw this in the airline industry. The ones who had a strong, healthy foundation, based upon their people came through much better. They were built for the long term."

"I would agree. I am impressed with your environment here. And your baseball diamond," I smiled. "Obviously it caught my attention immediately, but before we go there, I want to understand your position. Your title is Operations Manager. Can you define for me your tasks and responsibilities?"

"Sure." Mr. Anthony reached over to a bookshelf and grabbed a dictionary. "As you can see by my baseball wall, I like to define words. Let's start with the definition of operations and we'll build from there."

This concept impressed me. With the definition I can then determine how much of what Mr. Anthony does is defined within the definition, and how much is deviated. It was a good way to lay a foundation to build upon.

"Operation," Mr. Anthony read. "There are a few definitions; let's find the ones that suit what this department is based upon. Let's write it down so we can keep it in front of us for our conversation."

With pen and paper ready for dictation, I nodded at Mr. Anthony.

"Here is the first definition," he said. "Operation, 'a process or series of acts performed to affect a certain purpose or result.' Now that's a good start, but here is another, 'operation--the agency of a business organization that carries out planning and operating functions on an executive level.' Those two definitions are a good foundation."

Mr. Anthony waited for me to finish writing, then taped the paper to the side of his computer screen.

"Okay, now what?" I asked.

"You asked me what I do. I'd rather place it in the context of what we do, 'we' meaning the staff that works with me in this department. Let's look at the definitions. 'A process or series of acts performed to affect a certain purpose or result' and 'the agency of a business organization that carries out planning and operating functions on an executive level.' If we do this, we are executing what our function is. Let me break it down simpler in more defined terms for our business. But let me first say, I am sure many businesses have staff performing our functions, no matter what type of business it is. We are a sales organization, but it is no different in manufacturing, advertising, or whatever type of business there is. In a sales environment, we naturally have our sales department, which is responsible for sales and revenue. Now with what we sell, we coordinate the product that is being sold. Our product is a service, but even if it were something more tangible, like a car, furniture, or the manufacturing of such, you would still have the function of what we do needing to be executed. So, our staff bridges the gap between our sales department to our product or service that is sold.

"I could take forever breaking down every little detail. Our staff is responsible for day-to-day operations. We provide the ability for the sales department to have a product to sell. That starts by a process of a series of acts performed to affect a certain purpose or result. We are involved in every aspect from helping coordinate hiring, training, tools, and many other needs for both the sales and service departments. Our role doesn't stop there as we do the same for all departments that we have here."

"What other departments?"

"Well, obviously most all companies have accounting functions and technology functions, so our department is responsible in the same capacity to those departments also."

"Wow, that's a lot of responsibility," I said.

"Sure, it's a challenge. But with a really focused, purpose-driven staff, we can execute at a high level. Like I said before, when a product is sold, it must be delivered or executed based upon what it is. We plan all that out. In other words, we serve all other departments. It's important that we understand that fact. We play a fundamental role in execution of our success. Imagine in the car manufacturing industry that they must build cars, but then have them shipped to their dealers. All of this must be planned or there is no product to sell. We must do it without egos and realize that many times we have to pick up the slack. I remember reading about a successful football team that had a sign in their locker room that stated, 'Leave your egos outside.' Our staff has to do that. We must understand that our job is about execution."

"Does all that responsibility come with a lot of stress?" I inquired.

"It has its moments, but now it is a fun challenge. It took building the right environment and focus. I think you would find my staff enjoying their tasks and challenges. Actually this is why I created this baseball diamond on the wall, to define what is important to me and our staff. I combined items for both me and my staff to learn. Obviously, I show its importance by its visibility. It has had a profound effect."

"Is this something that you learned from Mr. Scott?"

"Mr. Scott inspired me by how he would list his focus out in the open. With his insight and management, we listed areas of need for me, as well as our staff. With that exercise I developed what you now see in front of you."

"Did you utilize baseball for a specific reason?"

"Actually, I did choose baseball for its significance on how the sport is played. You start at home plate, but to be successful in baseball, a player must make it around each base. Ultimately, you go around the bases to home plate again. So where you start is where you finish, if you are successful that is. With that in mind, this played a part on what focus and what words I listed next to each base. At home plate, I listed values and principles. Where you begin will be your foundation. No matter what other bases or lessons there are, I must always start at home. It is important to have a foundation of values and principles. Everything else builds from that. With values and principles as my starting base, I am more likely to succeed around the bases."

"And the other bases?"

"The other bases are pertinent challenges that I and my staff currently face. With Mr. Scott's help, I pinpointed these areas of focus. If I can improve in these areas, I can grow. Making it visible encourages our staff in participation so that we can all grow. It is not only the Operations staff, but our whole business. I think that will be evident as we work our way through the process."

"How did you choose the words for the bases?"

"Each base represents areas upon which we can improve and enhance our skills."

"Is their order important?"

"Yes, I did them around the bases for a reason, as there is importance of need and how they play into each other."

"Okay, can you explain more?"

"Sure. First base is "Anger and Danger." I've had a problem with anger. This affected how I would respond to others and how I made decisions, so this is dangerous. I cannot make it to second base without dealing with this issue. As I find success, I make it to second base to then be able to deal with Problems and Opportunities. Obviously anger and danger have to be dealt with before problems and opportunities. As I go through the lessons of problems and opportunities, I can then advance to third. When I am at third base, I am almost home. But with my experiences of each base and by playing the game, I have to deal with Knowledge and Change. What knowledge did I gain? What knowledge do I still need to gain? How did that change me? What changes are still needed? These are all valuable questions. As I succeed, I will make it back to home plate, values and principles. You see how that works? I can't succeed without starting with values and principles and also without finishing with values and principles. That is the significance of home plate. Where you start is where you want to finish."

"Why the definitions below? Why is everything defined?" I asked.

"That is a lesson I learned by raising my children. My definitions of things did not always match up with their definitions. For example, as my son was growing up, he would help me each weekend with the yard work. This included mowing, edging, trimming around flower beds, sweeping and cleaning up. When my son was in his early teens, it became his responsibility each week to do all the yard work. It didn't take long to realize that our definitions of yard work varied. He would just mow the yard. I would then have to tell him that it was incomplete. Well, then he'd edge it, but he still left out the other stuff. I invested in a simple chalkboard that I hung up in our garage to list the chores and a complete definition. So, yard work was 'mowing and edging the yard, along with trimming around the flower beds, completed by sweeping up all trash.' From that point on, when I expected the yard work done, there were no questions about it."

"Sounds like a good exercise."

"It is. But it didn't solve everything quickly. I assumed that exercise would educate my children to think before they did other things too. But I had similar problems with them cleaning the pool or washing the dishes. So soon I defined pool cleaning, 'vacuuming the pool bottom and sides of any dirt and debris, skimming the pool with the pool skimming net of surface dirt and particles, along with cleaning the pool filter baskets by emptying the pool catch baskets and washing them with the hose. Then testing the pool with a chemical test kit and adding necessary chemicals. Concluding with putting away of all hoses, poles, and equipment.' I added on later 'checking around pool deck and washing down when necessary.' With my daughter, who was responsible for dishes, washing dishes became 'thoroughly washing every dish with complete rinsing, emptying and cleaning of sinks, counter tops and cooking area, completed with drying of dishes and putting them away."

"Did this help?"

"Yes. I remember still having to define a clean room to my daughter and sometimes other things would pop up. Many times after you define something or a subject, you will then add to that definition over time. But something else happened that was just amazing to me."

"What was that?"

"Eventually my children started seeking out my definition on things on their own. I might ask them to do something and they'd respond,

'Dad, can you define that before I do it so I will do it correctly?' That amazed me. But you know, our staff has responded in the same manner. Human nature is amazing. The next amazing thing was that my children were then the ones adding to the definitions. They would say, 'Dad, I washed Mom's car today, and I think we need to start scrubbing her floor mats also.' What this showed me was this exercise grew them in initiative. Once again, employees have been no different."

"So the definitions are law?"

"The definitions are foundations to begin from. It allows no misunderstanding or miscommunications. Much like the exercise with my kids, we've had to add to the definitions from time to time."

"Before we go into each of the base definitions and their importance, is there anything else you wish to expand on?" I asked.

Mr. Anthony replied, "I want to emphasize the game of baseball and its significance to our discussion. Now I took you around the bases once. Obviously we wish to round the bases many times as that would signify continual success. Baseball is a team sport, so sometimes I may be stuck on first and need someone to move me over. If our team plays together, we'll keep advancing and scoring runs. We can add more or different subjects on the bases as we grow. The objective is to keep scoring, to keep advancing each other. If you've ever been to a baseball game, you know watching your team score is exciting—exciting for the players, coach, and especially the fans."

"Who are the fans on your baseball field here?"

"The fans are our customers, our employee's families, and our future employees. Customers like successful people. They like doing business with successful companies. Just as important, we want employees' families to cheer for us and to appreciate their family member's place of employment therefore becoming some of our biggest fans. Our fans are also our current and former competitors' employees wanting to be a part of our winning team. It happens that way in professional sports.

Players of other teams want to play for the winning organizations. They envy those players that do. Isn't that a great environment?"

"I would have to agree. Okay, take me through first base."

"Great, let's play ball! We start at home with values and principles. This is an important foundation to build upon. When we advance to other bases, we still have values and principles at home plate. Everything is built on the values and principles we start with. But what I also like about home plate is that it is also where we finish. Our objective is to score. In baseball, you drive in runs starting from home plate, but everything must be driven back to home plate to score and win. So, this ensures that even though we start with values and principles, we finish with them also."

"How does that relate to business?"

"In business, there may be challenges that present themselves that will give you the opportunity to not stay the course of those values or principles. Most of the time, these instances would be for short time gain. So, in understanding this symbol of baseball, we must finish with the same values and principles. Remember, in baseball, if you run out of the base paths, you're called out. That is not the result you want. Well, in business you may think you're getting a quick result but eventually you're called out. It will always present itself."

"How, and in what ways?" I asked.

"Let's first define values and principles. *Values:* 'a relative or assigned worth or importance; a principle, standard, or quality considered worthwhile or desirable.' So in essence, this definition says it is something we give worth to, something we consider quality. By saying it is a standard means literally we stand on it. I like the fact that the word principle is included in defining values.

"Look at the definition for *principle:* 'a fixed or predetermined policy or mode of action; moral or ethical standards or judgments collectively.' A principle is a predetermined mode of action. This means that when an issue arises in regard to that value, our principle or mode of action is already set. But the second part of the definition is that a principle is both 'moral or ethical standards or judgments collectively.' So because principle is used to define values, then a true value must be based on morals, ethics, and sound judgments."

"What about when you hear of people having bad values?"

"We hear that all the time. That is why I think defining things are so powerful. By placing moral, ethical, and sound judgment as a precondition, anyone with bad values must reassess their values. I question if maybe they really have no values."

"How would they have no values? Can you give an example?"

"How about a man or woman who is not faithful in marriage. He or she may claim they value sexual freedom, but where are the morals or ethics? Personally I believe they have no values. Truly the values they have are not based upon morals or ethics."

"Good point. Take me through values and principles, how you derived them and why."

"I believe the exercise starts with the individual. Personally my top values are God, my family, and then myself. Now on values, you can usually break them down more. On my value and belief in God, I value a balanced life that puts God first and never loses focus of that. On family, I realize their importance. I also value that balance. By having my family as a top value, I stay focused to keep that balance and to be a part of their life. Finally, I value myself. Included in that is my health, and also my appearance. How others see me also plays a role into that."

"Those are your values. How did they affect your principles?"

"With each of those values, work can play a role in them. I value my job and my success, but there are times I may get too carried away with the job and work all the time. So by realizing these values, I have to step back and re-balance. Now sometimes it takes my wife to draw me back. She knows I have these values, as I have shared them with her, so she'll just bring it up. No fighting or arguing has to take place. You see, because I've made her aware of my values, she helps me with them. This is the same in business. Because others know my values, they also help me with them. You'll find they also consider your values when making decisions. Now they could not do that unless they knew them, could they?"

"I suppose not."

"Mr. Scott knows my values, and he'll consider them when we have to work extra hours or have some kind of weekend summit. Because Mr. Scott has similar values, he encourages balance and has at times included our families in his final decisions. For example, we had all been working hard getting ready for our corporation's annual meeting. Mr. Scott saw a need for us to meet on a Saturday to further our preparation. Mr. Scott then had a dinner for our spouses that evening, which they really appreciated. It's things like this that makes my family a big fan of this company. When I came up for the design for this baseball wall, I knew to set it up would take some time, which I did not want to take away from my regular daily tasks. Because family is a value to me, I had my son work with me on it. We went to the store together to purchase the items. We cut out the parts, and my son even had a few ideas. My son enjoyed this as well as I did. He realizes his importance to me and really feels a part of his dad's life. What son doesn't enjoy following their father around his job, yet alone participating? I remember following my dad in his business. Your values show to others as they are witnessing those values in action."

"What would you say are some of the values that you put forward in business?"

"I would say I started with the same three, God, my family, and myself. This allows me to show respect in the same values of others. If I value family, I will work toward their balance also. Now obviously there would be many more, such as my job. I value my job and my employment, so I treat that with respect also. Now another would be the respect of others. So, if I value others' respect, I will show it by how I respect others. You see how it's reciprocal?"

"It sounds pretty basic."

"Three key values are trust, integrity, and honesty. It is important that I can trust others and others can trust me." Mr. Anthony grabbed his dictionary again. "Trust is defined as 'confidence in the integrity, ability, character, and truth of a person or thing. One in which confidence is placed.' Integrity is 'rigid adherence to a code or standard of values.' Honesty is defined as 'truthfulness; sincerity.' They go hand in hand with each other. Because these are high values, it is imperative I earn trust from others and be able to trust them. On integrity, the codes we adhere to are codes of morals and ethics which house honesty. Honesty is important in every situation, even at times when it might be difficult."

"What times is honesty difficult?"

"Honesty gets difficult sometimes if we have to reprimand. Reprimand does not have to be brutal and, in fact, can be done more effectively with tact. I value others' feelings, and I also value their knowledge of circumstances for their own improvement. So, we keep it simple, direct, and factual, then we state and acknowledge expectations. We confirm expectations, strategize on obtaining those expectations, and move forward. Within that process we lay out goals and follow up. Therefore, it is an effective process. With lack of honesty, we do not benefit the employee. In fact, I've said that very statement to an employee during counseling: 'Because I wish you as an employee to benefit from this process, I will be completely honest.' This is why it is also important to always do all employee evaluations honestly. If you're not honest or you sugarcoat areas, how can you be upset when that employee does not improve?"

"I see your point. I remember places I have worked where people's evaluations never looked bad, but no one received raises. Ultimately, no one advanced and the company was stagnant. Was that a result of lack of honesty?" I asked.

"It very well could have been. Obviously not knowing the other circumstances, I cannot comment on any other factors. But if we value having a strong company for all employees, then we have to stand on that value. You see, that's how values and principles work. Values help you define your principles or what mode of action to take. Everything must feed through that principle. For example, let's say that integrity is a value. A shortsighted goal could be achieved by fudging numbers, but because integrity is my value, my principle or standard will not allow me to do so. The mode of action becomes more automatic the more you practice it. The danger is not practicing it one time. Others witness that one action and it is very difficult to obtain their trust or belief again. What happens when you don't stand on integrity once, then at another time an employee does the same thing. Sure, two wrongs do not make a right, but you created the situation."

"Good point. What happens if you don't take a stand on your principle and others see it? Is it all lost? How do you get it back?"

Mr. Anthony replied, "If it happens you must call it what it is. Don't hide it. Confess it, acknowledge it, and condemn it. Honesty, as quickly as possible, is the only way to get it back. You'll see as we go through the baseball game stages of my personal growth and how it affected me, my staff, and other employees. You will also see why defining a foundation of values and principles are very important, and you'll add others, as I did. It is an exercise to continually take your situations and circumstances through your values and principles. The more you practice this, the more automatic it will become. Another important thing to remember is to watch your results. Your results will show you the quality of your values."

"Can you explain?"

"Sure. Remember, a value and principle should be based on morals and ethics. If our values are wrong or bad, we'll get a wrong or bad result. Evaluate your values and principles continually. We humans can fool ourselves on bad values. A value of hard work can at times really be selfishness. Continual evaluation can help define that. There will be more examples that we will identify I am sure, as we go through the process. Shall we?"

"Yes, we started at home but now we are running to first. Why is first base anger and danger?"

"I needed to make first base anger and danger because I've had to recognize that my anger is an area of needed improvement. In my position, I am challenged many times by circumstances created in other departments and by other individuals. Many times this would anger me and I would show that anger. Sometimes I'd become enraged. At times I'd say something demeaning about the individual. Our prior manager never confronted me on it. He allowed it. I suppose his attitude was to just give me distance, and after I would calm down, I would accomplish what I needed to accomplish anyway. But I did say some really demeaning things in my anger."

"What kind of things?"

"Terms like stupid and idiot, those kinds of words. I never considered the effect it had on others or on me and my management capabilities. By my prior manager doing nothing, it probably even increased. In a way it empowered me more."

"Okay, how have you come to terms with it?"

"When Mr. Scott took over, he discussed his values openly and allowed us to comment on his values and discuss ours. One of his values was the respect of others and to respect others, as respect must be reciprocal. Well, there I sat and agreed with him saying that was one of my values. It's funny, we'll claim a value, but we will fail to recognize that we're not living it."

"What helped you recognize that?"

"It only took one time for me to explode for Mr. Scott to confront me on it. He addressed me immediately. He reiterated his value of respect and reminded me that I too had said it was one of my values. He told me by the outburst he witnessed, I'd thrown that value right out the window. Values are easy when everything is smooth, but the true test of a value is when times are difficult. He said I just failed that test.'"

"What was your response?"

"I tried to rationalize my anger and say that this outburst was warranted and justified. I pointed out the situation that caused my anger."

"What did Mr. Scott say?"

"He stopped me mid-sentence. He said, 'I know your job is challenging. You would not be in this position if you were not able to handle those challenges. Looking at this situation, I can see how you would be upset. But being upset will not allow you to change your value. What your outburst did was disrespect other employees. I will not allow that. I know your history. When I took this position I was informed about each staff member and the comment on you was that you really knew your stuff, but you had a problem with outbursts. This tells me because you were very efficient at what you do as a department head your outbursts were overlooked or they put up with them. I will not. I'm here to help you. First, I value your knowledge and experience, but with that said, I will not compromise my values. I want you not only treated with respect but I want you respected. That is not always the same thing. A show of respect can be fabricated. So let's talk about your outburst and what I can do to help."

"Wow, what came up in the discussion?"

"At first I still tried to make excuses. I rambled with complaints about other departments, some legitimate, some not. Mr. Scott allowed me to ramble as he listened. He said some of my complaints were legitimate, and he thanked me for them, but some were just smoke screens. He said, 'An alcoholic cannot overcome or improve until he is able to admit that he has a problem. I need you to really take a good look at evaluating yourself. I will say this as directly as possible, I'm disappointed in your outburst and show of disrespect of others. I will expect and require a different attitude from you that puts respect first. Now as your manager, I will be happy to assist you in overcoming this situation. Your success is very important to me, and I value you on my staff. I would hate to lose you.'

"What was your response?" I asked.

"I was still a little defensive, but Mr. Scott saw that immediately. He said, 'I acknowledge your job is difficult. I also acknowledge that you accomplish your job with a high degree of success. But as we define your job, your job also comes with values. One of those values is respect. I have this job as operations manager which is trying and challenging because you are serving all departments. To serve others means to meet requirements or needs of others satisfactorily. This job must maintain the values we set forward. Mr. Anthony, do you want that job?'

"The rehire technique I heard about before! How did you respond?"

"I was quiet for a moment. Mr. Scott's technique and his directness got my attention. You know, it really earned my respect. I realized Mr. Scott corrected me, but did not belittle me. He was able to tell me that he was disappointed at my behavior, but did not attack me personally. He showed me I could be upset or disappointed yet still maintain the value of respect. After all, Mr. Scott did exactly that to me.

"I acknowledged that I did have a problem. Mr. Scott thanked me for acknowledging it. I then told him I wanted the position, and would work on the value of respect. I asked him how to work on my problem. Even admitting it to him was embarrassing."

"What did Mr. Scott say?"

"He told me personal acknowledgment was the first step and we all have things to acknowledge so we can improve. Acknowledgment is a step in humility. Humility is not a weakness but a strength. Taking that step in humility opens the door for improvement. Mr. Scott shared some of his experiences in the past. He explained that as he grew in humility, he became less embarrassed. The quicker he would acknowledge a situation he needed to work on, the quicker he improved. His humility then allowed him to even ask others for help. Mr. Scott explained this is part of the reason he places many of the very things he's working on himself on his office wall. He's acknowledging it to others, and in a way, asks for their help and support by doing this."

"So what did you do?"

"I asked for his advice. Mr. Scott said that I didn't have to run out and announce it to everyone. But he did suggest that I tell my personal staff and ask for their help and feedback."

"And did you?"

"Yes, I did. It was hard at first because of pride, but my staff really opened up to me. I found out how my outbursts actually affected them. I realized that there were times they wouldn't be open to me and would keep things from me out of fear. I realized that I inhibited their growth and our success. It was humbling, yet rewarding. I apologized and I asked for their help. I asked for them to be open with suggestions and corrections. I received so much out of that experience alone. I then came up with the idea for my baseball wall. I wanted to take the next step and acknowledge it to others. I did this by creating my wall."

"And what has the response been?"

"Very well received by my staff. They are all much more open now. However, when other employees saw my wall, I saw no drastic change in them or acknowledgment, but then Mr. Scott said something so true that set things into perspective."

"What was that?"

"He explained that others will look to see the change in me. They'll need to see it in my walk and talk. He explained he used to have a problem being humble. When he set out to change, he would tell people that he was trying to humble himself or he'd announce, 'I'm humble.' He realized that telling people he was humble was like a woman telling people that she was a lady. If she has to tell you she's a lady, she probably isn't. He said people will look for your walk. They'll not expect perfection but will recognize true effort."

"Wonderful. So can you take me around first base?"

"We started at home plate by setting strong values. If you are going to attack areas for growth or just business as usual, you need good strong values that are your foundation. As you move forward, your values will shape how you manage and develop or how you play the game. I put anger on first base as I knew it was hindering my personal success and our success as a business. If I could grow, develop and realize my weaknesses, I could improve. The value of respect had to be implanted in my everyday thought. Getting angry hurt my decision-making process. The dictionary definition, 'a feeling of extreme displeasure, hostility, and indignation or exasperation toward someone or something; cages; wrath; ire' described me. I realized I lost the respect of others. That is why the word *danger* is next to the base.

"The definition of danger is 'exposure or vulnerability to harm or risk.' My anger and outbursts harmed relationships. I'm sure my decisions in anger may have risked business. Around this same time, I had signed up for a faith-based course with my wife and one of the chapter titles was, 'Anger is one letter away from danger.'[7] This showed me how easily anger puts us in danger. I remember an old saying, 'A word spoken in anger cannot be erased. It plays over and over again.' So true. If I called an employee a name, I couldn't take it back. I could apologize, but my next outburst would only make my past comments play over in each employee's mind.

"Mr. Scott really helped me by his honesty and directness, as obviously those are his values and principles that he stands on. So, my process was day to day. I would get excited about each day and making it through with no outbursts. My staff was sharing more ideas and bringing situations to me quicker. In fact, they even spoke up when they disagreed which allowed them to become more open. Amazingly this communication helped us make better decisions. Other employees seemed to be more open and personable. I was amazed with how fun my job was. Make no mistake, we still had challenges, but it just seemed we enjoyed tackling the challenge instead of complaining about it. Our efficiency has really improved."

"You have three more words defined under *Anger* and *Danger*. Can you tell me about their purpose and importance?" I asked.

"Yes, meek, humble, and temperament. It started with Mr. Scott telling me humility was a strength. I had thought the opposite. I thought it was strong to be demeaning, vocal, and even arrogant. But I looked at the example Mr. Scott set. He walks in humility. He doesn't say, 'Look at me; I'm humble.' It just shows in his way of being. Because of his humility, he doesn't demand respect, he commands it. That's the biggest difference. In looking at Mr. Scott, I defined three things. One, Mr. Scott is meek. It's funny, but I always thought meekness was a weakness also. I thought you could walk all over meek people. Well, you can't walk over Mr. Scott. His meekness is a strength. He is actually more sure of himself.

"The definition of *meek* opened my eyes: 'showing patience and humility; gentle.'[8] That is not weakness. A patient person doesn't explode. A patient person is more open. I knew I needed to be gentle in my responses and reactions. Mr. Scott was a good model. Look at the way he told me he was disappointed at my actions. He was gentle yet more effective. His gentleness earns respect. So now when I'm faced with anger, I step back to remember my values. This allows me to take the situation through my principles and react in a much better manner. The results have been good, and as others are becoming convinced more of my change, it is becoming infectious. The word meek is my reminder to be patient, humble, and gentle. My values and principles are becoming more automatic."

"So what about the next word, humble?"

"Being humble helps round it out. Look at the definition: "modesty in behavior." Again, this isn't a weakness but a strength. A humble person doesn't shout and say, 'Look what I accomplished.' Accomplishments are like humility; people will recognize them by results. By watching Mr. Scott, I see how his humility helps others grow. Because it's not about him, others receive credit and try harder. Everyone trying harder is good for our business. Humility grows a good environment. I've worked for a manager who was just the opposite. Everything was about him. His behavior did not encourage effort, but stifled it.

"The final word is temperament because Mr. Scott would discuss with me the importance of managing with an even temperament. When I would get angry, people never knew which version of me they would get. This had caused many not to approach me or to keep things from me. I had been blind to it. Working on my temperament was important. Defined as 'the manner of thinking, believing, or reacting characteristic of a specific individual,' I wanted to work on my temperament and I wanted mine to include meekness and humility. That is why I included these three words together. Posting the words helps me and our staff. By employees seeing my focus, we earn their buy-in and their participation. I work on my even temperament daily. By this exercise, it's becoming more automatic."

"That is great stuff. How would you relate this to cause and effect?" I asked.

"Simple." Mr. Anthony replied. "My anger was caused by my pride, arrogance, and shortsightedness. I was blind to the effect. Because of my outbursts, I caused my staff and employees to hold back their communications, etc. So, the result or effect was that we probably didn't handle many situations as early as possible. Think about it. Situations will not hide themselves but will always surface. By the time I discovered the situation or someone else brought it to me, it was probably worse than it should have been. It made us operate less efficient.

"Another effect it caused was my staff and I lacked enjoyment of our jobs. One person can affect many. If your people aren't enjoying their job and feel like they are not a part of a team, your environment suffers as well as efficiency. My growth, as well as my staff's, was being held back. Other departments and their employees suffered. Our efficiency and productivity are vital to our business. I see it so clearly now as our correction, both mine and my staff, have caused the opposite effect. Our productivity and efficiency have improved productivity and efficiency everywhere. Individuals on my staff have grown in their roles. I've seen the cause and effect from both perspectives. I like this perspective better."

"Thanks. Would you like to take me to second base now?"

"Yes. Only after I pass first base may I advance to second. Home plate is values and principles. Only with the right foundation did I have enough success to make it past first base, Anger and Danger. I must be past Anger and Danger in order to conquer Problems and Opportunities. In all planning and decision making, we clearly need the best way to make the best decisions and make them quickly."

Mr. Anthony once again grabbed the dictionary and thumbed through a few pages. "*Decision* is 'the act of reaching a conclusion or making up one's mind.'[9] *Decisive* is 'having the power to decide;

conclusive.'[10] So, we have the power, but even more, it is exercising that power. How do we make good quality decisions decisively? The first thing we had to do as a department was to look at things from a new perspective. We make business decisions all day long. Most are within a normal day's operations, but what about decisions that come because of a problem situation? This is where, before, my anger would be a detriment. I made some decisions when angry, and I realized that I had to quit making rash decisions, yet still make good decisive ones."

"So explain more about the new perspective."

"In the process of working with Mr. Scott in dealing with my anger, he would call problems opportunities. He said if we attack the problem in the right way and come up with a good decision with success, we've taken the opportunity to advance, learn, and grow. We have even taken the opportunity to eliminate the problem from occurring again if we take advantage to learn from it. Also, many problems in our business are just situations challenging our growth and borders of innovation. He allowed me to see the opportunities they are. Mr. Scott showed me past examples of good things we do as a business that were born out of a so-called problem. This opened my eyes and helped change my perspective."

"How do you address the situation?"

"Let's go back to the baseball diamond. These definitions are foundational. Problems are 'a question or situation that presents uncertainty, perplexity, or difficulty.' We want to take that and turn it into an opportunity. Our definition of opportunities is 'a chance for progress or advancement.' If we've done that, then we've grown and can be better for that. Thus how we make decisions is very important. This is why I also list the definition of failure and success so that we truly know the difference. Failure is defined as 'the condition or fact of not achieving the desired end or ends.' Naturally we wish no failures; so, a success is defined as 'the achievement of something desired, planned, or attempted.' Yes, success, that's what we want."

"But don't failures occur?"

"Failures do occur, but our job is to make sure that our failures are not detrimental to the business. There are other kinds of failures that occur with innovation and experimentation of growth. But whatever they are, the first thing we must do is call it what it is. Then we take the opportunity to learn from that failure so the next time we have a success."

"Have you had any such failures, and what did you do?" I asked.

"Yes, we had one such failure that as we looked back on the circumstance, it allowed us to address our decision-making process. We had a challenge on the service side of our business due to growth. We were hit with an opportunity presented by our sales staff that stretched our capabilities. In short, I had one client we could not provide our service to according to the time frame needed. Well, the solution seemed simple. We were able to bring in an outside associate who is independent of our company to cover that service. This associate would do so in our name, and everything should be transparent to the client. Things did not go well with the associate in servicing the client, and naturally and rightfully the client was upset. Remember, all the responsibility fell on us. We had a challenge and we thought we had met the challenge but failed. It's funny, but the solution seemed so simple and our decision was made quickly and decisively, but it was not the correct decision. When the situation occurred, I was angry, and I believed we were not responsible. Mr. Scott helped open my eyes and worked me through the process. I was able to see our error and how differently the decision would have been."

"Yes, but wouldn't that decision have taken time?"

"Actually the decision would have taken about the equal amount of time. The process is not consuming but it is complete. You see, we made a rash decision, not a decisive one."

"How did Mr. Scott work with you?"

"Mr. Scott had just taken over. At that time, I was stubborn and blind in my anger. Mr. Scott confronted me and patiently talked with me. In my stubbornness I made the statement that we shouldn't be challenged with those circumstances again. Mr. Scott replied, 'Challenge is a part of growth. If we wish not to grow, then we'll eliminate those challenges. If we choose to grow, then we'll be faced with challenges. I believe we grow or we die. I choose to grow. We should never stay stagnant. What we must do is find a way to best meet our challenges.'"

"What was that way?" I queried.

"Mr. Scott was patient. It was me who did not accept responsibility. I told Mr. Scott that we couldn't be blamed as we had done our best. He simply said, 'I'm not here to blame, I'm here to fix. As we fix, we'll discover reasons why things occurred as they did. Failure isn't falling down. Failure is staying down. If your failure is derived from effort, then let's just define a better way to utilize that effort.' Mr. Scott went through a method to make decisions. He learned it long ago from a counselor on behavior modification who used it to teach troubled youth their decision-making process in life. Ultimately that's our objective: to make the right decisions. It's a universal decision-making process. We don't need to shy away from challenges and decisions. We want to improve the way we go about them. We do not look back in anger or forward in fear. We need to look around in awareness."

"What is the process?" I asked.

"It's really basic. Number one is defining the problem or challenge and our goal. We ask, what is the problem or challenge? Then we ask, what do we really want? In this example, our challenge was that we were short on our service side to keep up with our sales challenge. We defined what was needed, a service. Our goal was a successful service with a satisfied client. We used a chalkboard when going through the process. After a while, it became natural to staff.

"The next step is information and insight. We ask and define: what do I know? We also make assumptions: what do I think I know? This has proved a valuable step. Another question that I never considered was others' points of view. I'm not talking about taking a survey, but for me, it's my staff. Occasionally it's Mr. Scott's or another employee's. Other's points of views have many times added value to our decision. On our failure example, I had another point of view given that I simply did not consider. That view had value."

"Apply this step to your example, please," I requested.

"What I knew is what service was needed. I also knew our service side personnel capabilities. When it comes to our assumption, well, we made no assumptions of our associate's capabilities. Had we made assumptions, we would have looked a little closer at our scheduling of our service personnel. You see, we had one of our service personnel who would have been perfect for that service need. Because we made no assumptions, we simply did not look at this. The associate we hired simply could have covered the service that this employee was assigned to, as it was a much more basic service. I have to admit I probably didn't consider it because I really didn't want to change my schedule. Foolish pride is what that was. Pride is a real killer."

"Well, what about others' points of view you mentioned?" I asked.

"The sales person who helped create the challenge, which was really an opportunity, made a suggestion in considering that alternative. I was close-minded to others' points of view, so I never even looked at it. I simply thought my job was to just cover the service. I thought I did my job. Looking back, I see things more clearly.

"The next step is to consider what are the alternatives and consequences. So we ask, what choices do I have? That question would have allowed us to look at other possibilities, and we would have seen the better choice. So the second question is what will happen for us, the client, and our business? It allows us to look for an answer where the final answer for each is, 'This is the best decision.'"

"That's valuable. Are there more steps?" I queried.

"Yes, the next step is to choose, plan, and do. We have our choices. Now we ask, what's my best choice? We also ask, what's my best plan? You see, once we make our choice, the plan is how we are going to implement and execute. Both questions must be considered.

"The final stage is to evaluate. We need to evaluate on successes and on failures. On each we learn and improve. So we ask, what was my goal? I know we asked that in step one, but we ask again. Human nature can tend to change the answer to meet our needs or the decision we made. Ultimately the goal should be the same as in step one. If it changed, it usually means we compromised. We ask, are things better or worse? Did we create an opportunity or close one? That's important to know. Another question is, will this meet our needs over time? In other words, were our decisions ones that we can stand on for future decision-making? This is what helps build solid decision-making. Finally, we ask ourselves, what have I learned? Hopefully we learned our successes can teach us, but our failures we must learn from so we can conquer and eliminate. Too many people believe you only have to get yourself up after a failure, but if you don't take it through this process, the failure was in vain. We must ask, what have I learned?"

"Good point. So what have you learned?

"I learned humility and the strengths that come with it. I learned where we went wrong. I learned a useful tool in making decisions. I learned it doesn't take any longer to make a good decision than a bad one. I've learned that the more I practice along with my staff, the more automatic the process is. Mr. Scott summed it up after teaching the process by saying that good judgment is built brick by brick from painful lessons learned."

"I truly see the benefits of Mr. Scott's giving people the benefit of his time. Mr. Anthony, are we ready to go to 3rd base?" I asked.

"I think we've rounded second and we're headed to third. Each base lays a foundation to the next. The foundation starts at home plate, the first building block, as setting values and establishing the right principles are instrumental to success. For me, it was to address my anger and avoid danger.[11] With success at first base, I was able to build up to success at second base. Making decisions with a clear mind, not rashly nor in anger, and with a valid thought process allows us the best chance for victory. This whole process actually defined third base for me and its value, 'Knowledge and Change.'"

"Can you expand on that for me?"

"Certainly. In the past I always wanted to effect change on my anger problem. My past managers wanted me to change, but no one supplied the knowledge. *Knowledge* is 'understanding gained through experience or study.'[12] Now that can be my experience or others. Mr. Scott has been instrumental in sharing his knowledge in helping direct my change. Sometimes it may also be knowledge in what we are blind to. I was blind to the negative effect my anger had on our business, my decisions, my staff, our employees, and even myself.

"What's important is Mr. Scott just didn't lay out the facts but he walked me through the process. His exercise allowed me to see it for myself, which was a humbling moment, but added more value. Make no mistake, Mr. Scott let me know in no uncertain terms that I needed to change, but it wasn't just a demand. The definition for *change* is 'to transform.'[13] Well, I needed to transform. Too many times we demand change but we don't provide the means. Mr. Scott taught me that knowledge is the vehicle for change. Without knowledge, any change would have been fabricated. Sure, I could have stifled my anger, but it would have still been there. In order for me to change my anger,

I needed Mr. Scott's help by giving knowledge to change my behavior. I also enjoyed his motivations, which were my rewards. He was very patient and positive. Mr. Scott was factual when he needed to be."

"So how did that help you with problems and opportunities?"

"Much in the same way. You see, Mr. Scott didn't just hand me the method to make a decision and say, 'Here, do this from now on.' He coached me through the process. With the coaching, I saw good decisions formulate. More importantly and valuable to me was when Mr. Scott walked me through a failed decision. Think about successful coaches in sports. They're successful because they are teaching their knowledge."

"How does this work in management?" I asked.

"The very same way," Mr. Anthony said. "If we desire change in behavior of an employee, we attack it with coaching and teaching. That's why coachable employees are the key. You can have the smartest employee in appearance, yet if they are not coachable, they will not change. This is crucial in building a team. A team must have only coachable employees. Each person we work through our process. We supply knowledge, give them the benefit of our time, and we utilize rewards or consequences. Throughout this time, we are being confrontational, as we confront all things. But our confrontation is factual, not negative. Throughout this process we are able to evaluate. Only because we are active in these ways can we continually evaluate. Knowledge is the vehicle for change. If you desire change, define the knowledge needed. Coach it and teach it. Your involvement is motivating and helps in team building. Your involvement sets a clear trend on business desires. Imagine that knowledge spreading throughout, and it does. This builds a sense of team. You'll see ownership and employees helping other employees."

"It sounds so reasonable and like such a good environment."

"It is! Look, knowledge and change are third base, but I'm going home. Everything I do or we do, goes back to home plate through our values and principles. We start with values and principles and we finish with values and principles. Remember, we want to keep playing and rounding the bases. Also remember, baseball is built around coaches. You have a third base coach, a first base coach, and a coach in the dugout. My point is they are coaching during the game continually. That is the "secret" to a successful team."

"I would have to agree with you. I thank you very much. Mr. Anthony, in closing I would like to ask you four key points that you would like to leave me with."

Mr. Anthony said, "Well, let's go around the bases as we make these points. Number one, values and principles are a key with cause and effect. It's imperative to have the correct values that establish the correct principles, and then stand on that principle. As long as you stand on your principles, you'll have the direct result of your values. This will allow you to continually evaluate. If you consistently do not get the desired effect or result, then you have an incorrect value and incorrect or incomplete principle. So, re-evaluate and adjust. But if you compromise your principle, then you cannot do a true evaluation. Another danger is others have seen your compromise, and your value and principle will seem less important to them. In a sense, you've cheapened its value. Now it is okay that as you stand on your principle that you then re-evaluate to adjust the cause, which you tweak from there. Be honest, straightforward, and confront it. Others will see this as you putting worth on your values and principles and their success."

He continued, "Number two, know that humility is a strength, not a weakness. This was taught to me by added knowledge, which allowed me to change. I had to realize that a man's language is an index to his mind. This knowledge and perspective allowed me to see how others see me. This humility allowed me to be honest in evaluating myself and to show a desire for change. As with any behavior change, it takes effort and continued practice on good behavior. It's not automatic. But as I practice healthy behaviors, my feelings will follow along. It helped with Mr. Scott's assistance and his coaching. But my humility allowed me to build a support network of others to help. I was able to communicate my desire and effort to improve. My wife assisted at home and a couple of my staff assisted here. Only pride would have held me back in the past. Sometimes we believe because we're someone's superior that we have to be superior. That's a farce. I found that my support network became more supportive and shared in the success. I also found they saw me as real and human. Many supervisors or managers don't want to be seen as human. That's a mistake.

Mr. Anthony paused, then continued, "On number three, I wish to re-emphasize how easy it is to be decisive, but with a good process. The process becomes a habit and instantaneous as we implement it daily. Others will think in the same manner. The mistake I made is that I believed to be decisive I had to limit myself of good tools, whether they are people or other resources. And finally, number four is to embrace change, whether within yourself or in circumstances. Things change in our businesses continually. But as I learn to embrace change, I hunger to grow in knowledge. It's like me filling my car up with gas. My car is the vehicle that gets me places. Knowledge is my vehicle for change. Sometimes change isn't cheap. It will cost you a death to the old in order to experience a birth to the new. But knowledge helps you realize that, and you'll desire it."

"Thanks, Mr. Anthony. I now would like to meet with Mrs. Kendall, who is listed as your service manager."

"Sure, let me walk you to her office."

CHAPTER FIVE

THE CURRENT AND THE ROCKS

Mrs. Kendall was an attractive, well-dressed woman with a pleasant countenance and a presence of professionalism. Her office was very organized with shelves and desk trays. Her walls had pictures of her family along with pictures of employees and employee functions. Another wall had awards. At the top left side of her wall was a small mirror, with a message above that read, 'Have You Checked Your Reflection Today?' Underneath was a printout that said, "If you can look at the reflection in the mirror at the end of the day and feel good about your day, you've passed the test." Another picture was a split picture of a NBA basketball coach whose team won the world championship and the team holding up the championship trophy. Underneath was a printout that read, "There are two views of success, whose are you focusing on?"

The next picture was a group of people rock climbing. Underneath was a printout that read, "If your climb was easy, maybe you chose a hill instead of a mountain." The next picture, one of two people hugging. Underneath was a diagram that said *gratitude, thankfulness, appreciation*. Mrs. Kendall also had two poems hanging on the wall. The first was directly beneath the mirror and its message. It was apparent the poem went with the picture of the man looking in the mirror.

Have You Checked Your Reflection?[14]

Look at me each morning
Tell me what you see
Are you starting the day
Who you want to be?

And as the day goes by
Come take another glance
Are you staying true to yourself?
Or have you changed by chance?

At the end of the day
Look, am I what I expect?
Can I leave today with assurance
I lived my values with respect?

Let's always look in the mirror
Because each day is our test
Do we like what we see?
And are we doing our best?

Challenge your answer
Get past the perception
Do you trust what you see?
Without any exception?

Author Unknown.

The next poem was underneath the NBA coach and team, "Employees Mimic What They See":[15]

I know I can wait
Because my boss comes in late
He's never on time
So why should you mind

He shows no respect
So what do you expect
So why the surprise
That you caught me in lies

When he never takes blame
It's always the same
So that's now my default
It's never my fault

Talk's in the air
It's different in here
Here is one I can approach
He's my new coach

Can't believe what I see
He's focused on me
I like this indeed
He fulfilling my needs

I am having success
I truly am blessed
This job is so fun
It's my number one

It never did seem
That we'd be a team
But now we perceive
That we can achieve

Each day I am grinning
That we each are winning
I never would guess
That we'd be the best

Author Unknown

Mrs. Kendall's wall struck me with the impression of a person that really cares for her employees. "You are listed on Mr. Scott's organizational chart as the Service Manager. Can you briefly explain that title?" I asked.

"Sure. The title Service Manager means I manage the employees that provide our service. Because we sell a service, we must have employees perform that service. If we sold a tangible product, I would be the product manager. Either way, my responsibility is that we deliver what was sold to our customer. Our objective is to deliver that service above our clients' expectations and with complete satisfaction. We realize that we are an instrumental part of the business process because we are the product. As we deliver and maintain consistent high quality, we become instrumental to the sales process. Our success is vital for repeat business from clients. We are vital in the forming of partnerships. We realize that our sales staff helps create this process, but our security is to advance it. We are an essential part of the team. My responsibility is to maintain that and always work to improve it."

"Wonderful, thank you," I said. "Each manager has shared with me how they play into cause and effect in their management philosophies and areas of needed growth or advances. I see on your wall here where you list your beliefs and focus much like they did. Did Mr. Scott ask you to do such a wall?"

"No, but learning from his example I witnessed how valuable and effective it is," Mrs. Kendall replied. "I saw my colleagues utilizing the concept in their own way and their staff's growth from it. With the evidence of good results, I became affected in wanting what they had. I did ask Mr. Scott for direction and counsel as well as the other department heads. I then finalized it with the team leaders of my staff as they were very willing to participate. I now see how they take ownership, and it permeates through our whole service department."

"That's great," I said. "With utilizing your staff, how did you arrive at the end result?"

"I had them share their views. Seeing things from their perspective was extremely valuable. The exercise gave each of us more respect for each other's views and job task. Seeing things from each other's perspective showed us that we as individuals were not the only ones with challenges or burdens. It expanded us to share each other's burdens, which brings better results. It was this exercise that brought to light the number one issue on our wall, 'Have You Checked Your Reflection?'"

"I am glad you pointed to that as that is my next question. Can you explain more?" I asked.

"Yes, but let me first give a quick example. A few years ago I used to tell myself that I was fit and trim. I believed my face was thin and my stomach was flat and that I was in good shape. A friend saw a photo of me from this time and she made the comment, 'Wow, you were a little plump back then, weren't you?'

"She meant it as a compliment because I am thinner now and in good shape, but it made me examine the picture again. There I was in the picture smiling back with a plump face and a stomach. I had convinced myself that I was slim and trim, yet I realize now that others saw me as the picture showed, plump face and stomach. I wasn't being honest with myself or as the poem says, 'get past the perception.' The truth is I didn't want to see it. But I did honestly want to be fit and in good health. However, by not being honest with myself, I held myself back from achieving my full potential. Now a year or so after that, I realized that I wasn't fit and found fitness, but I do regret it didn't happen sooner. So, back to my sign on my wall, we feel it is important first to ask ourselves and our employees to really look at the person in the mirror, whether it pertains to work or home, because if we do not see our reflection truthfully, we cheat ourselves of our full potential."

"How do you implement it?" I asked.

"Well, the exercise we did to come up with our areas of focus helped us arrive at implementation. In our sharing to determine the areas of focus for our department, we realized we saw each other differently. It's eye opening. We each agreed to step back and look at ourselves in the glass. This then allowed us to ask ourselves good questions."

"Like what type of questions?"

"The basic questions derived from the poem, 'Have You Checked Your Reflection.' First, who does this poem say you must satisfy by trusting what we see and why? Think about that. We must satisfy by trusting ourselves first. It allowed each of us to reflect on what satisfaction is for us. This question allowed us to list what we wish to achieve in life, both at home and at work. By knowing this, if we cheat on anything which takes away from us achieving items on our list, then we are not being honest with ourselves and hurting ourselves first."

Mrs. Kendall continued, "The next question is 'What does it mean to be honest with yourself?' We found that being honest with yourself was calling things for what they are. In that picture three years ago, I was out of shape, but I told myself I was fit. By doing this, I didn't achieve my full potential. What if my unfitness took a toll on my health? Results of my dishonesty can cost me and others around me. The third question is 'How do you cheat the person in the mirror?' Well, by not being honest, I cheated myself out of fitness. In a job you can cheat yourself from advancing and growing. A person that tells themselves that they are spending enough time with their children but truly are not, are robbing themselves of joy, plus the joy their children experience. How many times have we told ourselves, 'I wish I could do it over?' but we can't."

I nodded for her to keep going.

She continued, "The fourth question is 'Why is it important to be honest with other people?' Through the honesty of others, we each came to see a truer reflection of ourselves. Mr. Scott manages in the same manner. We let each other know as well as our employees that we'll be honest. Mr. Scott uses factual, not negative, and it's very effective. My friend's comment about me in the picture was factual yet revealing. Only honesty done in a way not to belittle, but to assist, will grow yourself and others.

"Our fifth question is 'How do you judge whether a person is honest or not?' This can be a hard question, but it is one that as managers we must ask. It is one also in society that we must ask, as parents and just as everyday people. As managers, we must ask ourselves this question. First let's remember the philosophy that trust is verified, not blind. Our everyday task and actions allow us the verification of that trust. That action or behavior brings results. If those results are consistent with the right behaviors then that also brings verification. Finally, if we believe we have a problem with dishonesty, then we confront it. This allows us to correct it or eliminate it. Remember, it is rewards or consequence."

"Thank you. I like the message. With this focus, how do you further implement it into your environment to make it an everyday thing?" I asked.

"It starts with the hiring process," Mrs. Kendall said. "It doesn't start after someone is hired, but as we are going through the process, we communicate and we look for it. From there we express it daily. With our employees, we've created workshops that we have every other month or so. We cover many different subjects, but we'll weave in the 'have you checked your reflection' concepts continually. We let employees share stories on their successes and failures. Their honesty really drives it home to others. Within the workshops, we create exercises that are fun yet reinforce the message. But no matter what, we ask each employee to ask themselves ten questions as they look at their reflection at the end of the day."

"What are those questions?" I asked.

"Let me go through the whole list first, then we'll go one question at a time."

My Reflection in the Mirror

1) Do I have an attitude to win and achieve success?

2) Do I believe I am doing everything today to be successful?

3) Am I doing all that is asked of me?

4) If there is more I can do to assist myself, my employer, or other employees, am I doing it?

5) Am I giving a complete effort today with no shortcuts?

6) Do I value others, their opinions, and their advice?

7) Did today go as well as I had planned?

8) Am I satisfied with today?

9) Will I give a complete effort tomorrow?

10) Will I try to improve tomorrow over today?

"That's the list for each employee to ask themselves as they look into the mirror each night. Naturally we could have thought of many more questions, and many do, that would only help them more. These basic ten questions are a good 'reflection in the mirror' exercise."

"Great, let's take them one at a time," I said. "Number one, 'Do I have an attitude to win and achieve success?'"

Mrs. Kendall nodded. "Here we desire each employee to contemplate and reflect on their attitude. How was their attitude today? Did they error in poor attitude at any time? What about any time that they were upset, even for a moment? This moment of reflection can be eye opening because many times we do not realize there was a time when we got upset. The reflection brings that out. We wrote the question as present tense and not past tense, for as a person's attitude is a continuous thing; with this, we desire a winning attitude to be continual. Now while utilizing honest reflections with any of these questions, it allows us to call it what it is. We then confront it and make a conscious effort to improve. Without asking these questions, we become blind to any area of needed improvement. A daily look in the mirror is a powerful tool."

"It is," I agreed. "Now let's go to question number two. 'Do I believe I am doing everything today to be successful?'"

"Ask yourself that question," Mrs. Kendall said. "If the answer is no, then what didn't you do? Many times we may try to wiggle around that 'no' answer and rationalize why we didn't do something. I am sure there are times we procrastinate and put something off until tomorrow. With this question I reflect what else could I have done today? Ask yourself, 'If I lived today over, what else would I have accomplished?' That's a good question at the end of the night."

"Excellent. Now question number three. 'Am I doing all that is asked of me?'"

"We ask a lot out of our employees, but a lot of what we ask is truly left up to them. It's true that trust is verified, but that may on occasion be after the fact. If we allow employees time to study and advance, are they truly taking advantage of that time? If not, they not only cheat themselves but also our clients as well as our business. Many do not realize that they are cheating their fellow employees who value that time and desire more. An employee may have natural gifts and therefore do not do all that is asked of them. Perhaps they are holding back their personal growth as well as our company's."

"Number four asks 'If there is more I can do to assist myself, my employer, or other employees, am I doing it?'"

"This one is a simple reflection. If I could have utilized more help, did I ask for it? If there is a question, need, or something I am lacking, did I speak out? If not, why? If I didn't, I may believe that only I suffered, but once again my employer suffers as well as all other employees. Is there something I could have done to help or assist my employer or another employee that I failed to do? If so, what is it? My reflection will allow me to plan to do what's needed the next day. Is there something I wanted to bring up to my manager? Did I see an employee doing something today that I could have helped them in which would have brought improvement? These questions generate active thought for betterment. There is much we fail to realize until we reflect."

"That's so true. It's a very simple thought process." I agreed.

"Yes, it is," Mrs. Kendall agreed. "These ten questions only take seconds each day. The more we practice them daily, the more they become habit. The habit of reflection is good and allows you to make improvements."

"True," I said. "Now let's go to question five. 'Am I giving a complete effort today with no shortcuts?'"

Mrs. Kendall said, "This question can play into some of the previous ones asked except we could answer yes to the previous ones and then come to question five and answer no. This takes honesty, as does each question. So here when one is reflecting, they either honestly believe they didn't take shortcuts and that they put forth a complete effort, or they realize any areas they did take a shortcut. Once again, perhaps they are gifted and didn't study or learn as was asked of them. That's a shortcut. Perhaps they didn't give a complete effort in helping or teaching others. Perhaps they had something to say to me and watered it down. If so, they not only cheated themselves, but cheated me and possibly others. There is much more that the reflection can bring out with each question."

"Well, that brings us to question number six. 'Do I value others, their opinions, and their advice?'"

"As you look back on the day, ask, 'Did I value others? Did I show them the respect I desire? Did I give them the time of day?' 'Did I go out of my way to be personable?' You see, it's not only giving them the time of day, but we may be avoiding others unknowingly. So, did I go out of my way to be personable? I hope to answer yes each day. We need to look back and reflect. Are we approachable? How did I react to others' opinions or advice? If I'm not receiving their opinions or advice, then why? It might be because of how I acted in the past. Or once again, did I seek any out? I find that a person who seeks opinions and advice is believed to be approachable by others and will receive some daily. Small corrections or insights can make drastic improvements."

"I've known people that others will not approach because they are not open to opinions or advice," I commented. "The sad part is this person is the one who suffers as they seldom improve and actually become blind, if not arrogant, to their ways."

Mrs. Kendall nodded. "That's actually what will happen. So look at that person in that glass at the end of the day and ask yourself that question. You will then improve yourself."

I agreed. "Okay, question seven. 'Did today go as well as I had planned?'"

"Well, did it? It's a simple question, isn't it? Or maybe you don't plan your day. That can be one of the answers. Or when you plan your day, did you plan for a good day? Did you give it much thought? This will come out in your reflection. But also ask, 'What would I change?' Is there anything that you would eliminate? What was the cause of that result? These questions will have you planning your days to be effective and productive. As we reflect each day we improve each day."

"Number eight looks very much the same as seven," I stated. "Number eight asks 'Am I satisfied with today?'"

"In some ways it does seem the same except when it's all said and done, even if there are areas to improve, are you satisfied? Can you go to sleep tonight satisfied that you achieved progress? Sure you may do some things differently, but it's still okay to be satisfied. But if you're not satisfied, make a mental list why, if not an actual list. Is your effort tomorrow going to make you satisfied at the end of the day? That should be your conclusion."

"Thanks for explaining that. We're on number nine now. 'Will I give a complete effort tomorrow?'"

"Do you see how the order of the questions progresses and builds on each other?" Mrs. Kendall asked. "Many may say this question is a given 'Of course, I will.' But by asking yourself each day, you're reminding yourself each day. This sets in determination. Now if your answer is no, then why? Are you unhappy? Can you change this status? Sometimes an honest reflection may bring the determination that you're in the wrong job for you. That's a wakeup call to change."

"That brings us to our last question. 'Will I try to improve tomorrow over today?'"

"To sum it all up, will I make that conscious effort to make tomorrow better? With my reflections, will I take the steps forward to improve? Now if today was considered a good day, then challenge yourself to duplicate it. But ask what could I do to improve? Set out to make tomorrow better. You'll find yourself enjoying your days more, not only with this question, but also with all of the questions. In one of our workshops, we encourage our employees to do the same in their personal lives to be full and complete. This exercise helps. A satisfied employee is much easier to be around at home, but it is also important they prioritize and keep their family at the forefront. Questions like. 'Did I show my wife love and respect today?' Or, 'Did I spend quality time with my children?' Or, 'Do my children know I love them today?' I once stopped dead in my tracks with this reflection and went and tucked my kids into bed and told them I loved them. We value our employees' success here and at home. I believe we show it."

"This is a great exercise, but why do you have this first?" I asked.

"Attitude is everything. This is the building block of everything that comes after. We have created a healthy attitude. It breeds the right environment."

"Let's look at the next picture and message on your wall. Are the people significant - the coach and the players? Or is their significance their roles?" I asked.

"I would say their roles. I chose this picture as a personal preference, as I followed this team as a fan in the 1980's. Even today I'm a big fan. My husband's friends think he is lucky to have a wife who loves sports." Mrs. Kendall smiled.

"The statement associated with this picture states 'There are two views of success; whose are you focusing on?'"

"There are two views of success. One view is my own personal success. The second view is the success of those that are the team.'Whose are you focusing on?' is a profound question. I say that because our focus is on the team. Simply stated, my focus is on the success of our employees and staff. If I focus on my success, I become shortsighted or blind to others. True long-term success comes by focusing on what it takes for the team to succeed. This takes becoming involved and knowledgeable to each individual. If you create this environment, you'll have an appreciative team, knowing that your focus is on their success. This coach had five championships in ten years. The other years they were very much contenders to win, but what brought this coach success was not focusing upon him or on what would make him look good. He realized that by focusing on his individual player's success that the team came together to be successful. Their success naturally brought him success, but this formula was long-term. That's the key to building this way.

"Shortsighted managers or coaches will focus on themselves. Sure, everyone wants results, but shortsighted managers or coaches make it all about them. Many autocratic styled managers or coaches have had quick success but usually long-term results fade. This NBA team excelled as a team. Over that ten-year period, they even made difficult decisions on players. But because they knew their coach's focus was truly on them, they knew it was for the better of the team. Their coach had their trust. Managing employees is no different. Now I have personally worked for both types of managers. The difference in the environment has me working harder. If you enjoy your work, the team environment, and respect and trust your manager or managers, you will naturally work harder. You'll find yourself more dedicated."

"How do you instill this?"

"I help my staff focus on our players, as I do myself. I evaluate their success based on those factors. Our employees' development is very important. Since Mr. Scott took over, we have had several employees get promoted outside this location. We've become a source of people development to our corporation. A shortsighted manager or coach would not want to lose anybody. A coach whose focus is on the player would understand that others growing breeds a stronger environment. Those that have gone on to promotions we hold up as examples. Our corporation looks upon us favorably, so our focus has brought Mr. Scott success. Funny thing is that when we lose someone to a promotion, we always have good people to fill those rolls. Tell me, would you rather work for an employer that had no growth opportunities or one that continued to have growth opportunities?"

"That's a no brainer. Obviously the one that continually has growth opportunities would excite me. I think I would naturally work harder at what I do." I stated.

"That is exactly my point. That's the environment this creates. That's the environment that helps sustain success. Focus on your employees' success and yours will come naturally. It creates a strong, healthy and enjoyable environment." Mrs. Kendall smiled.

"By interviewing the other managers, I am aware of many ways that you develop people here. I understand about giving people the benefit of your time, rewards or consequences, trust yet verified, confrontation as a benefit, factual not negative, and many of the other methods. I appreciate each one. But I've always believed that developing people is an art. So out of all these tools, what stands out the most as a key to developing people?" I queried.

"I remember listening to Mr. Scott answer a question on how our location develops so many good people for corporate promotions and he answered, 'With all the patience in the world.' Now all the methods we utilize are instrumental, but Mr. Scott stated two things: patience and empowerment. We must have patience to grow individuals and to allow them to falter at times. We use our methods to coach that individual through the process. But with that growth, we must empower them with challenges, knowledge, and tasks, and so on to bring them along. As Mr. Scott develops us, he'll delegate, which is empowering us. But Mr. Scott does state that true delegation is giving someone what they are ready for. I've seen past managers' delegate, but what they truly did was just load someone up. If there is no coaching, accountability, and follow through, then there is no learning or advancement. Remember, the person delegating must assume responsibility, not deny it. All of our methods are designed to utilize our people skills. Mr. Scott once said that if an employee gives him all their effort, he'll give them all his patience. Mr. Scott lives that daily. This doesn't mean there are not times that Mr. Scott or any of us must come to a decision on an individual, but our process executed consistently clearly brings that determination to light."

"Thank you, Mrs. Kendall. Now I notice that you have a poem hanging up that says, '*Employees Mimic What They See.*' Why do you display it?"

"I believe the poem is self-explanatory. Go through each line. What we show our employees each day has a direct reflection on how they grow, act, and succeed. I believe so strongly in this message that I display it as a continual reminder to me and our staff. We're not always perfect, so a visual reminder allows us quick correction. Seeing it each day also helps maintain our mindset, so we stay consistent. Second, I believe that by showing it to our employees it makes us accountable and makes them appreciative. Any time your employees are appreciative, you've grown your sense of team and enhanced your environment."

"Thanks. Do you have any other comment on this topic before we go to the next?"

"Only to remember that your peoples' success is your success. I'm here to help people be successful."

"Excellent. Let's go to your next sign and the rock climbing picture. 'If your climb was easy, maybe you chose a hill instead of a mountain?' What message are you trying to portray here?"

"If you look at the wall, we started by first challenging everyone to take a look at themselves. The process of self-evaluation is a strong foundation to build upon. The next step was the focus and understanding that true success is the success of your people. So this is understood and lived by myself and our staff as well as the other managers, but our employees see it and appreciate it. I desire our employees to expect it as the norm. When they do, you'll have a loyal, enthusiastic employee. With those foundations established, then it is our duty to challenge and assist our staff and employees to set high expectations. This is very much our job to help and do. So, the message here by the statement is to challenge yourself on your expectations. One must evaluate their goals and desires. We help and assist with goal setting. We put processes in place that sets high standards, but we also put the support mechanisms in place to help assist."

"Is there a special way you go about it?"

"First we speak it. We communicate high expectations in the hiring process, then through the training process, and then live it each day. Miss it in any of these areas and it will have a negative effect on obtaining consistent results. Now I would say the next step is what you believe.

"Remember the movie *Stand and Deliver* where a schoolteacher in Los Angeles believed his students could do better? This school did not have a track record of success as many accepted the environment of mediocrity. This teacher believed otherwise and set high expectations. He encountered resistance, but he taught or brought the students through the process of looking at that person in the glass. Next he showed and communicated his focus and efforts on their success.

The teacher was there to serve his students. He taught, coached, and encouraged them. With this foundation he was able to get the students to believe in themselves and to believe in high expectations. The process of believing is a key and a valuable process. Remember, if you think you can't make it, you're probably right. These students then believed, and that opened the door for the teacher to assist their growth. The teacher helped set high expectations, challenges, goals, and shared his vision continually. His vision focused on each of their success, and he spoke his vision daily. More importantly, he then showed the steps to obtain those high expectations, no matter how challenging they were. Whether it was studying harder, reading more, or helping each other, he was there to coach throughout the process. One thing that I like to point out as a belief that I have is that this teacher did not have a standard teacher's mentality."

"What's a standard teacher's mentality?"

"A standard teacher's mentality is that every student cannot get an A. Some must get B's, C's, and some must fail. The old mentality is that if everyone received A's then the teacher is not doing their job. Now how backwards is that? Isn't it the teacher's job that their students' succeed? This teacher believed more could succeed. He believed they could excel higher, and they did."

"So how do you change that mentality?"

"First you must confront it. Then you need to speak and communicate that you believe differently and that you expect differently. You will utilize all behavior tools. This teacher used rewards or consequence. He showed that trust was verified. This teacher truly gave the benefit of his time. Behavior modification is no different with school children as with adults. Now a lazy teacher could just give out the answers to their students, but this teacher taught study habits, and he taught that high expectations are a challenge. If he did give the answers, he would then educate on why it was the answer. Therefore, their understanding grew as well as their success."

"What other steps do you take?"

"Part of giving someone the benefit of your time is helping develop realistic expectations. From there, you lay out what steps those expectations require. You coach, participate, and monitor the process. You set a clear vision on what each stage of success looks like. When or if those results stray, you coach and correct as well as encourage. You utilize all tools within cause and effect."

"Is there any special way you guide them through?"

"Yes. Our job is to help maintain their focus. Take the example of a leader of white water rafting trips. This person leads the group as well as instructs them. His job is to help deliver learning, enjoyment, and ultimately their safety. Now if you have ever seen people white water rafting going through the rapids, you'll see an exhilarating event. I always wondered about navigating around the rocks. How does one teach that? I asked and the leader's reply was that he taught how to navigate the raft and how each one affects it. But he also explained that if you stare at the rocks, you will naturally drift toward the rocks. So, he teaches everyone to focus on the current. After all, the current was the vehicle taking them to their final destination and success. When one worries and focuses on the rocks, the likelihood for danger and failure are increased. Well, business and employees are the same way. Our job is to teach safety but to focus our employees on the current, not the rocks. Focus on the vehicle leading you to success and you'll avoid danger."

"But don't employees have to know about the dangers?"

"Sure they do. We teach that before the trip, just like they do in white water rafting. If they start to stray toward danger, we correct. But our belief is that if we can keep employees focused correctly, they can achieve high expectations. The wrong focus will not achieve this. There is a profound difference between caution and too much focus on danger. We must teach and recognize the difference and coach through it. Now, like in rafting, sometimes some failure may occur. But by our training, we maintain safety and then take that opportunity to learn. This instructor said that most of the time if they hit rocks or someone flips out of the boat, the person almost always admits they focused on the rocks. By evaluating, one can admit the circumstance, then learn and make corrections and then move forward. Some may struggle or be hesitant to move forward while others make the right change of focus. Our job is to evaluate that process. That brings me to my next illustration."

"Great, what is that?"

"I recently read where a hired guide took a group horseback riding in the mountains. The leader explained that on part of the trip the path was about six feet wide going along the side of the mountain. On the other side was a cliff with a rather long drop. The leader explained that those riders who focused on the cliff, their horses would automatically walk along the cliff side. Those riders that did not focus on the cliff, their horses would walk along the mountainside. When they reached their destination, the group shared their experiences. The riders who rode along the mountainside spoke of the beauty, the clear blue sky, and the forest. The riders who rode next to the cliff spoke of the cliff, their fear, and how long the drop was. Each reached the same destination but had different experiences. The riders that had caution knew the cliff was there, but didn't allow that to affect their focus. The other riders allowed caution to turn into fear and did not have an enjoyable experience. It's our job for our employees to have the best possible experiences. Good experiences grow expectations within oneself and help us challenge ourselves more. A bad experience can be a setback and cause us to lower our expectations. On this trip, the leader explained how those with the bad experience wanted to turn back or not go on to the final destination. It affected their expectations. If one is straying, we must recognize it to correct, coach, and encourage continually."

"Is there a method of doing that?"

"Well, it is not my intention to dwell on horses or compare people to them, but situations on training can correlate in behavior, whether human or animal. I also read where someone asked a trainer how to teach their horse to comfortably cross narrow waterways. The horse was fine crossing water that was six feet wide or more. The trainer explained that the horse must have had a bad experience in the past crossing a narrow waterway. The trainer explained that it is the owner's job to overcome the horse's natural instinct or the aftereffects of a negative experience through patient training. The trainer stated the owner first must build a strong foundation or establish a leadership position with their horse so that the horse will respect and trust the owner. This process must be followed to correct negative experiences. Obviously it is better to eliminate negative experiences from happening. But when they occur, we must realize them and put these steps into place. Now look at these steps. Number one, build a strong foundation. Two, establish a leadership position. Then three, earn trust. Isn't that our process? The tools of cause and effect are designed to do exactly this."

"I see and agree. You mentioned helping setting goals and sharing vision continually. Can you explain more?"

"Sure. Let's talk about setting goals first. One important factor in assisting an employee on setting goals is not just to set them to our desires. The employee must share ownership of that goal. If I force what I believe their goals should be, then that employee's ownership is lost. Sometimes that could be the very rationale in their mind if their goal is not obtained. They might rationalize that it really wasn't their goal anyway. We must meet and share in this process. The employee shares their goals and their views on why they believe their goals are reasonable and also show tangible means of obtaining them.

"We as managers share our views and communicate whether we think the goal was too low or too high. If there are no tangible means of obtaining the goals, then we'll address why and make it more realistic. Within the process, we define our reasons and expectations. Our experience over time has shown that as an employee has been through this continual process on the two views on goals, the employee's view and our view, that the views are actually very close.

"This process can only be successful with us as managers having close knowledge of all the facts, not blind knowledge, which can only be obtained by our close, daily participation with each employee. That is why the whole process of cause and effect is valuable."

"Excellent. I like it. Is there more?" I asked.

Mrs. Kendall continued. "We witness that the employees value our participation and appreciate that we are so closely involved. We use this process continually, whether we are defining small goals or long term ones. We encourage our employees to set personal goals that involve their outside life and family. Many have their personal goals hanging up in their work area. These may include a home purchase or vacation location. We have celebrated many times when personal goals have been obtained.

"There are times when we may re-evaluate a goal. We'll look at results and share our views of the factors involved. The employee will also share their views. At this time, we may adjust the goal to make it more realistic. That may become easier or a more challenging goal. Once again, as the employee works and lives in this environment we actually see that goals are being set higher more than lower. The process is a continual process and adjustments are made continually at the proper time of need, not waiting until total completion."

Mrs. Kendall paused and then continued, "I believe the importance here is that we don't follow a blind process. I remember under past management we'd ask for goals of something and employees would give a blind answer. On several occasions, a manager wouldn't accept that employee's goal and would impose their expectation. This process allowed for no involvement, no coaching, and ultimately no ownership. Our goals were obscure and, if met, it was more out of luck than out of a good process."

"Thank you. Now can you define vision for me?" I asked.

"Vision is foresight or unusual foresight. The vision only becomes unusual as the process you utilize creates the vision's accuracy. Each employee has their vision of success at work and at home. These visions come to fruition by conquering their goals. This is why a good process in goal setting is so important. If you have ever read Zig Ziglar, he teaches to start with the end in mind. So, with their vision, the end would be what it would look like, feel like, smell like, and any other factors. From there you work backwards and break it down by needed steps. This helps define goals, and once again this is why a process that allows us as managers to be knowledgeable in the areas that are tangible in creating the results is valuable.

"I admire the golfing legend Jack Nicklaus. I have read that he envisions how he will accomplish making it to the green for each hole. He looks at the challenges, such as yardage, water or sand traps, and the layout of the fairway. He envisions where he will hit his first shot and where it will land. Jack further envisions where he'll shoot from there and once again, where it should land. He determines what it will take to achieve each shot. He thinks on how high to hit the ball, or how much spin, if any, and what club he needs. His vision allows him to back up and define everything it takes to obtain his objective. By utilizing this exercise, Mr. Nicklaus has had tremendous success. But at any time that a particular shot is different than his first vision, then the adjustment for the next shot is an easier process. Because he has envisioned each shot, evaluation is easier and then adjustments are easier. The thing I like in the process is with an easier evaluation and adjustment process, corrections are less intimidating. Corrections are a natural part of the process. These processes we teach, coach, and speak continually."

"Yes," I nodded. "Anything else to share?"

Mrs. Kendall stated, "Another important factor is to teach and coach employees to continually speak their vision. We work individually or in workshops, and our team environment grows as employees encourage each other. This builds on our team aspects and also creates employees challenging other employees, which creates higher expectations and accomplishments. What I like most is employees helping each other and sharing in the accomplishments."

"What do you do about your visions for individuals and your visions for this department or business as a whole?" I asked.

"It is much the same way. I share and define my visions with tangible breakdown. I speak with the end in mind and everything that leads to it. So, whether it is on an individual or on our department, I communicate the vision continually. It is our job as managers to help the focus of our employees. We must coach, teach, and communicate continually to achieve the goals that determine that vision. We must communicate adjustments and corrections along with the sharing of feedback, which is invaluable. One year we set a vision to win a company-wide award. We spoke the vision, we utilized the process and defined goals and objectives that would lead to that vision's success. As a team, managers and employees worked to maintain focus on obtaining each goal and in making adjustments and corrections. As a team we took ownership and responsibility. That year we had tremendous success, but we did not win the award. Now our success was evident, and we very easily could have been the recipients, but because we were such a strong team through this process, we kept the vision and the focus and won the following year. From that time forward, we have maintained strong consistent success. The process has taught us and developed our behaviors. Our true vision is our success, individually and as a team."

"It seems like the award was confirmation on the process, but truly your continued success, I believe, confirms that more," I said.

"Absolutely, and that is how we see it, teach it, and speak of it. You see, if the award were the only goal, we would have won and then possibly would have slipped in our performance. Now the vision of winning assisted in determining goals, etc., but we spoke and learned that continual success is the ultimate goal. That's the difference from a dynasty to a one-time winner."

"Good point. I'm reminded of my old high school tennis coach constantly sharing his vision of our team and breaking it down individually. We developed into a strong team and won our league. When I look back at it, I remember how the whole process was motivating and how his words had power." I smiled.

"Yes!" Mrs. Kendall replied. "What we communicate and speak has power. As we speak and define our visions continually, they then become embedded in our minds. Hearing that we can accomplish goals and obtain our visions helps us grow to believe them."

"Can you now take me through the diagram on gratitude, thankfulness, and appreciation?"

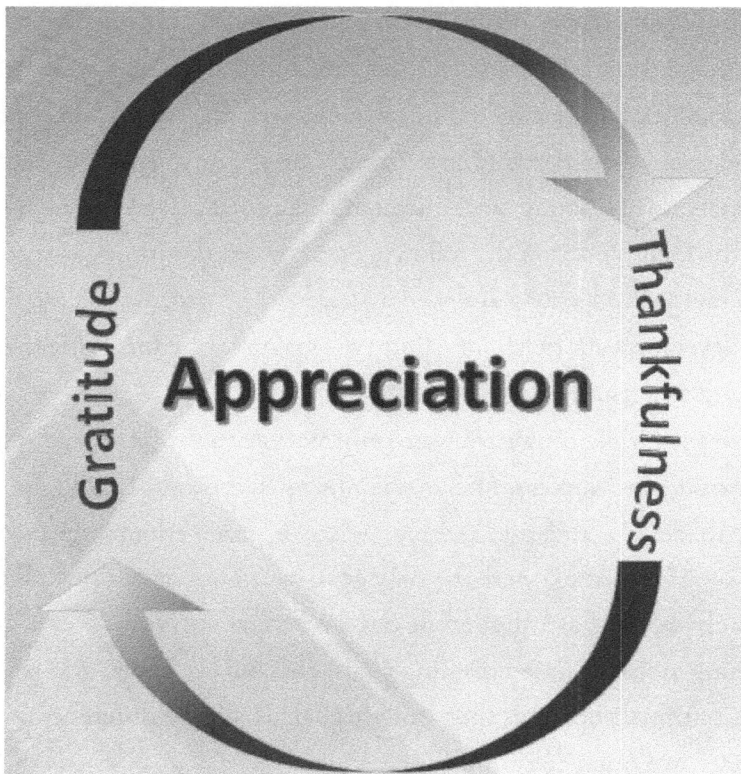

Gratitude → Appreciation → Thankfulness

"It's really very simple. You see our whole process on how we manage leads to this. We want to show appreciation to the point that our employees know and believe in its legitimacy. Our goal is for our employees to feel the same. In thinking about appreciation, we then ask, how do we obtain it? Our vision would be to have management and staff that show and share their gratitude through thankfulness with the culmination being our employees feeling appreciated. We back up and break it down. If appreciation is the effect we want, then let's break down its cause. Gratitude is the feeling and thankfulness is the expression. We draw it as a circle as it evolves one to the other continually. The more gratitude I feel, then the more thankfulness I express. As these factors rotate, what builds is our appreciation. This is a continuous cycle that builds and spreads.

"Each day we look for things to be grateful for. We teach others to do the same. With our gratefulness, we then express our thanks continually. Many bosses don't realize that a simple 'Thank you for your work today' goes a long way. It is the least expensive way of team building, yet the most effective. Of course we expect hard work, and we get it. The power of thankfulness builds spirit, morale, trust, and ultimately appreciation. Simple things can make a huge difference from an enjoyable day to a tiresome day. We say thank you daily and often to our employees. Our staff and employees know Mr. Scott appreciates them, and his expression of thankfulness is genuine."

"I wish to express my thankfulness to you, Mrs. Kendall. I have asked each manager to sum up our meeting with four things they would like to leave me with. What four things would you like to express?" I asked.

Mrs. Kendall said, "There are some added points I would like to include in our conversation. I'll review my messages on the wall with my additional comments."

"Great, I appreciate that."

"I wish to expand on our first message on the wall. 'If you look at the man in the mirror at the end of the day and feel good about the day, you've passed the test.' This starts in the hiring process. Ask others to review what they see. As we instill this exercise in employees, we teach to work through preconceived perceptions. Perceptions can alter what you believe you are seeing. In our workshops, we work in pairs or groups to get others' views and perceptions. A view is to describe factually what you see; a perception is the reasoning from a belief on why that view is that way. Because many perceptions are preconceived and set in our minds, it can actually change what we look for in our view. We may see it differently or we actually subconsciously look for particulars. If I have a perception that someone is unhappy, I would look for those signs. Perhaps I would look for how they hold themselves up, a frown, or I would think I would hear it in their speech. This is why our workshops are so valuable. Our workshops unify us as a team and teach us to work together and trust each other. Our environment builds encouragement. So, we start by looking at the man in the mirror, but we help each other also. Do I see in me what you see in me? Why do you see that in me? We realize through our exercises how environment plays a role in our views and also our perceptions."

"How is that?"

"Think for a moment. If I were to tell you I witnessed a man slashing a woman's stomach with a knife, what would you first think? Then what if I told you that man was a doctor and the woman his patient and that the woman was pregnant and the doctor had to take the baby to save its life. Your view of that man would be different than before. Instead of the man being a bad man, you'd view him as a good man and a hero because the environment and the circumstance change the view. I am sure that just by the environment of me being a manager of a department gives others a preconceived point of view. So, our exercises help find the whole person."

"Your workshops sound like a valuable tool. Mrs. Kendall, what would be your next point?"

"Our next message, 'There are two views of success; whose are you looking through?' My point here would be that as you focus your concern on others' success, this breeds a reciprocal pattern of behavior. By showing my focus and concern on employees' success, their concern grows for mine. People will grow in loyalty and go the extra mile even when it's not asked of them. They see your concerns and efforts as genuine and become appreciative. Their appreciation builds upon that winning environment. One thing all managers must realize and grasp is that your people are a reflection of you and the environment you've created for them. If you're lazy, they become lazy. Beware of the manager that complains that all his employees are lazy. I remember once being at a conference and hearing a manager from another location complain that his people were useless. This seemed to be a common complaint each time I came into contact with this manager. Now what was that manager saying about himself? Understand, if you desire your employees to work hard, make sure that you're working hard. If you desire their timeliness, then you must be on time. Naturally you'll deal with those that may deviate from your example through behavior modification, but your team as a whole will reflect you."

"I agree," I said. "I remember a manager who would leave early every. Eventually the employees wanted to do the same. This manager became frustrated and pointed out that we were paid to work until a certain time, but the reality was our belief was that he was paid to work till that time also. Our next manager did the opposite; he worked hard and into the late hours. In a short time, the employees naturally progressed to giving a full effort until actual quitting time. The changes just came naturally."

"That's my point," said Mrs. Kendall. "I believe each of us can look at past examples we've had personally. That's a powerful tool."

"Okay, now your third point?"

"The third message, 'If your climb was easy, maybe you've chosen a hill instead of a mountain?' My point here is it's okay to give your employees the answers. Now what we must realize is how to give the answers to where it is constructive and a benefit. For example, my husband signed up for a carpentry class to learn as a hobby. To graduate, there were thirteen tests to pass. The instructor would just give out the formulas required to pass. He stated, 'Just learn the formula and you'll pass the test.' This frustrated my husband because by just memorizing the formula, he did not comprehend why the formula worked. My husband met with the instructor and explained that if he understood the formula's logic or why it worked, he would not have to memorize it. By understanding the logic, my husband would come to the answer logically and understand the whole equation. Why does it work? What's the logic behind it? Now those are valuable answers. You see, it's okay to give the answers if your objective is to teach. My husband's instructor's objective was for his students to just pass. After his students passed, many still knew little about carpentry. What type of experience do you believe they had? We seek the best possible experience for our employees. If it benefits the learning experience, then it's okay to give the answers as long as you educate the steps to the answer along with the logic and the why."

"But shouldn't people find their own answers?"

"Sure, on many experiences. But if you're teaching a child to stay away from a cliff, you're going to give that child the answer. You'll explain what would happen and the dangers of the cliff. I don't think you'll let that child find their own answer. Many times a manager who never gives the answer is just a lazy and poor manager. Giving the answer allows us to educate and coach. Anytime you create coaching opportunities you win. Your employee grows as well as your environment."

"Wow, I like the concept. What would be your fourth point?"

"My final point really covers all four of my messages. I assume it really covers management and how we manage. My final point is not to allow your prejudices to taint your observation and objectivity. We all have things we like and things we dislike. We have beliefs, needs, and desires, which all come into factor daily. So with that, it is important not to let our prejudices taint our observations and objectivity."

Mrs. Kendall continued, "I'll tell you a story from a book I read by Norman L. Geisler and Frank Turek.[16] The book is faith-based, but this example is fun. The story is about sixteen-year-old Johnny. Johnny came down from his bedroom and stumbled into the kitchen to get a bowl of his favorite cereal Alpha Bits. When he got to the table, he was surprised to see that the cereal box was knocked over and the Alpha-Bits letters spelled out 'TAKE OUT THE GARBAGE--MOM' on the place mat. Recalling a recent high school biology lesson, Johnny didn't attribute the message to his mom. He'd just been taught that life itself is merely a product of mindless, natural laws. Thus maybe the cat knocked the box over or an earthquake shook the house. No sense jumping to conclusions. Johnny didn't want to take out the garbage. He didn't have time for house chores. This was summer vacation and he wanted to get to the beach. Mary, a girl he likes would be at the beach."

Mrs. Kendall continued, "Johnny's friend Scott liked Mary too, so Johnny wanted to get to the beach early to beat Scott there. But when Johnny arrived, he saw Mary and Scott walking hand-in-hand along the shore. As he followed them at a distance, he looked down and saw a heart drawn in the sand with the words 'Mary loves Scott'. For a moment, Johnny felt his heart sink, but thoughts of his biology class rescued him from deep despair. 'Maybe this is just another case of natural laws at work!' he thought. 'Perhaps sand crabs or an unusual wave pattern just happened to produce this love note naturally.' No sense accepting a conclusion he didn't like! Johnny would just have to ignore the corroborating evidence of the hand-holding."

I smiled and Mrs. Kendall went on. "Comforted by the fact that principles learned in his biology class could help him avoid conclusions he didn't like, Johnny decided to lie down for a few minutes to get a little sun. As he put his head back on his towel, he noticed a message in the clouds on the sky blue background. 'Unusual cloud formation,' Johnny thought. 'Swirling winds perhaps?' No, Johnny couldn't play the game of denial any longer. 'Drink Coke' was the real thing. A message like that was a sure sign of intelligence; it couldn't be the result of natural forces because natural forces have never been observed to create messages. Even though he never saw a plane, Johnny knew there must have been a skywriter up there recently. Besides, he wanted to believe this message--the hot sun had left him parched, thirsting for a Coke.

"This story hits home with my final point of not allowing your prejudices to taint your observation and objectivity. In the story, Johnny didn't want to believe what he observed. Johnny lost his objectivity, and his prejudice of what he had believed or been taught is what he held to. You see, it's important that we as managers do not allow our prejudices to do the same. I've witnessed a manager who really liked an employee to the extent that they refused to admit what they observed about that employee. That manager's desire for that person to succeed allowed that manager to keep that employee longer than they should have. Because this manager lost their objectiveness, an environment developed from the other employees of resentment and lack of trust. The same can occur but with the facts in reverse. I have also witnessed a manager dislike a person for reasons not related to the job task. The important point is to always seek to be fair and objective. We develop strong communication with managers and with employees. It is with this communication that we have been able to build honesty in feedback to each other and to receive that feedback objectively. Once you establish this as a foundation, then it's easier to build and expect the same from each employee. Accountability starts with you first."

"Thanks, I appreciate your insight and your time." I stood up and shook hands with Mrs. Kendall.

"You are welcome, and I thank you. By your interest, I've been allowed to share. Each time I share, I grow. So for that opportunity I thank you."

"You're welcome," I said. I felt funny being thanked, but I also felt appreciative. It made me reflect on the discussion on thankfulness and gratitude. From there I excused myself and headed back to Mr. Scott's office for our closing meeting.

Chapter Six

WHAT COACHES DO - THE FINAL INTERVIEW

M r. Scott was on the sales floor and immediately made his way over to greet me. "Let's go in my office," he smiled warmly. "I trust your interviews went well?"

"Thank you for this opportunity," I stated. "I am enthused and energized by this experience. I found each manager professional and respectful. They each carried themselves well, and seemed well grounded and concerned for their employees. What impressed me the most was the focus on enhancing the best environment possible for the employees. I can see that each manager truly believes that focusing on employees' needs and development will ultimately create a successful business. They genuinely care, take a personal interest, and do the things necessary to support, train, and grow each individual employee. I must say, Mr. Scott, I am impressed. In fact, I would say I am amazed."

"Amazed?" Mr. Scott said. "Isn't that what coaches do?"

"Excuse me?" I asked.

"Everything you described, as well as everything that you witnessed and experienced, is what successful coaches do. The problem with the business environment today is they believe a manager in business is different than a coach. To create our ultimate desired effect, a successful business, we realize the best cause is being a coach. Once again, this is defined by cause and effect."

"I believe it certainly works," I agreed. "If you don't mind, can I ask you some wrap-up questions?"

"Absolutely. I ask for your feedback also. This exercise can be beneficial to both of us."

"Wonderful. When and how did you come up with your philosophy about managers being coaches?" I asked.

"It grew over time with the realization of cause and effect. Whether we truly know it or not, we break things down in our head constantly to determine their causes. Over the years I worked for several different managers of different philosophies. When I determined where I had more success, enjoyed my job, was challenged to learn, experienced growth, and obtained goals, it was always for the managers who took an interest and coached. Over time, as I managed, I have witnessed that as I coach employees, I have better consistent effects. Through the process I would see that coaching can change behavior to what is desired. Desired behavior brings desired results. Coaching legend Tom Landry once stated, 'A good coach will make players do what they normally would not do so that they would become what they always wanted to be.'"

"Tom Landry certainly got the most out of his players and for so many years," I agreed.

"Yes, Landry realized each player's dream was to be successful at their position, contribute to the team, and be a part of the team's ultimate success. He also knew that most individuals will have to change behaviors to obtain that success. Human nature has pride and ego, so we tend to fight behavior change. Many times we think we know better. Tom Landry used all the methods of coaching to create desired behaviors to help make his players become what they always wanted to be."

"I have seen some sports teams who have individuals who like to draw attention to themselves. In those cases, it is all about them, yet some of those teams have had success. What do you say about that?" I asked.

Mr. Scott replied, "Yes, they may have some success, but not consistent long term success. We even see teams packed with all stars, but because of individualism they don't win consistently or they win ugly. Now some may say, 'What is wrong with winning ugly? You're still winning!' I remember a quote from columnist Robert Novak who said, 'The trouble is that a team that wins ugly sometimes starts losing.' His quote referred to basketball, but it is the same for all sports, and especially for business. If you're winning ugly, it is imperative that you are coaching through the process to change behaviors to create a consistent successful environment."

Mr. Scott continued. "I recall an American Express commercial with Duke coach Mike Kryzeski, known as Coach K, who stated, 'I think of myself as a leader who happens to coach basketball.' Coach K realizes that he is a leader first. That is the first part of being a coach. Then he said, 'Coaches don't win championships, players do.' This shows why Duke has been so consistently successful. Coach K's focus is on his players' development. He realizes and acknowledges their importance, therefore realizing the importance of behavior modification. Because Coach K realizes these top two priorities, he knows it is not about him, but about each individual player. As he has focused on their success, it has brought team success. You can see that ultimately it resulted in his continued success."

"I do. Autocratic managers and managers whose focus is all about them receiving the credit seldom have long term success. I see that coaching is the most successful method. However, isn't coaching continuous and burdensome?" I queried.

"Yes, it is continuous, if not, you'll lose consistency," Mr. Scott answered. "If coaching is not continuous then things created by that lack of consistency will become burdensome. Consistency makes it easier. Think about consistency in coaching sports. It's not burdensome, it is simply what you do as a coach. I have an essay on coaching, rather poetic actually, from our company newsletter that discussed the correlation to business. I think you'll like it."

Mr. Scott handed me a piece of paper with the title "Coaches."[17] It read:

Last night, I went to a high school football game. As I enjoyed the game, I couldn't help but draw the parallel between the sport and what we do in business. More specific, I watched the head coach and the assistant coaches and how they parallel our managers.

I watched on every play how each coach was attentive to what their players were doing. While on offense, they watched for each detail. After each play, they would critique some players, some aspect, or the play itself. I realized this is what coaches do.

I watched as the offense came off the field and a coach critiqued and role-played with his line-men, preparing them for the next time they had the ball. I realized this is what coaches do.

I watched how a coach kept his team excited. How he complimented the good and kept his players focused. I realized this is what coaches do.

I saw a coach continually work with his kicker, even though he was very good, practicing, practicing, and practicing some more. I realized this is what coaches do.

I watched that while on defense, the coaches would inspire their players to be aggressive, yet smart. I realized this what coaches do.

I watched as the other team started driving down the field. The coach, because he was prepared and knowledgeable called a different defense. They stopped their opponent. I realized this is what coaches do.

I watched, on two separate plays, the coach tried trick plays. One failed, one succeeded. I realized this is what coaches do.

I watched when they scored how the team shared the excitement. He was creating a sense of team and congratulations. I realized this is what coaches do.

I watched as a player fumbled the ball. He came off the field with his head down. The coach stopped him, raised his head, and told him to get ready to have the ball again showing that player that he still had faith and confidence in him. I realized this is what coaches do.

I saw the team get flustered, confused, and disorganized. The coach called a time out, settled his team down, and got their heads back into the game. I realized this is what coaches do.

I watched the other team. They were behind by two touchdowns with two minutes left, yet still playing with intensity. How could they believe they could still win? I realized this is what coaches do.

I saw the same players, with ten seconds left and no chance of winning, continue playing hard, they knew they were preparing for tomorrow, and the next game. I realized this is what coaches do.

I saw discipline in the players, and discipline in the coaches. I realized this is what coaches do.

I watched and it was clear that each player had accountability. They knew they would be measured to this. I realized this is what coaches do.

I thought about great coaches and inspirations. I remembered stories about coaches like Dick Vermeil, working hard, long hours, thinking more dedication could make a difference. The next year he won the Super Bowl. I realized this is what coaches do.

I watched how the coaches provided leadership and guidance. They showed they cared and took a personal interest. I saw the respect they earned from their players. I realized this is what coaches do.

"That is wonderful," I said, handing the paper back to Mr. Scott. "Coaching is before, during, and after the game. It's continual and all the time. In sports and business."

"Exactly," replied Mr. Scott. "Other management philosophies focus on reports too much and fail to coach. Reports are important and beneficial because statistics point to areas of strengths and weaknesses. But statistics usually means the game has already been played. By coaching continually, you have a better opportunity of establishing your desired behavior patterns that enhance the opportunity for desired results. You are shaping what the statistics will be. By coaching, you'll witness more detail and will be able to respond. Clearly the best time for changing and correcting behavior is as it occurs, but also walking the person through the good behavior with coaching instructions explaining the processes and why. We as individuals respond best to this environment."

I nodded in agreement. "I have worked in environments that are so focused on reports that it's hard to get help when needed. What would be your advice to management in this environment?"

"My advice would be to step back and refocus. Reports are important and in some businesses mandatory. Step back, ask yourself what can we do to make coaching our priority, and reports secondary, and still accomplish both. Unless we first decide to make coaching a priority, we never will. In fact, we'll use the burdens of reports as an excuse. This cycle will never end. But if you make coaching a priority, then you'll grow your people. From there you'll grow your business. Only with growth can you open more opportunity. Now I understand that at first it may be difficult. It might take extra commitment from management working extra hours to do reports at an earlier or later time. But by coaching you're then creating a solution by growing your business. By growing your business, you then can rework the reporting by additional personnel, assistants, secretaries, etc. Understand this is a must no matter what is interfering with your management teams' ability to coach."

"What about situations where you might not be comfortable with the managers you have at the moment? You want to make changes but know that it might take some time?" I asked.

"That is a very real scenario," Mr. Scott stated. "I could come up with a hundred more reasons on why I might as the top manager become reluctant to have my managers coach. The true reality is even if each circumstance is real, we must not use it as an excuse to not have us start coaching. To coach the managers, you have to coach your employees. You have to be involved.

"An article in Chief Learning Officer[18] magazine talked about a study done by a Harvard University professor to determine how variations in lighting and humidity produced differing levels of employee productivity in a manufacturing plant. When the light increased, productivity went up. Since rules of effective research dictated testing more than one condition, the experimenters also decreased the intensity of the lights. Again, productivity improved. Similar studies were conducted with humidity and later with psychological aspects such as group pressure, leadership style and working hours. Regardless of the variable that was manipulated, productivity was shown to increase. The key discovery was not which conditions most maximized productivity; rather the studies eventually concluded that the productivity of workers increased simply because the researchers were paying attention to them. The improvement in productivity by the personnel was created truly just by showing interest in them. The insights gained from these studies changed the development of organizational leadership. The researchers learned that productivity could be maximized when employees felt as though their needs were being considered by receiving attention for their work. This phenomenon became known as the Hawthorne Effect (the name of the factory where the study took place was Hawthorne Works). Paying attention to our human assets produces tremendous results."

"Let me make sure I follow," I stopped Mr. Scott. "What you're saying is even if you do not have the management team you desire at the moment that you still need to start coaching. Simply by paying attention to employee needs, you will increase productivity. Correct?"

"Absolutely!" Mr. Scott replied. "Quit making excuses and start coaching your managers, and coach along with them. The simple reality is employees appreciate the effort and attention. Sure they may recognize that some managers are better coaches, but employees appreciate the effort that you put forward to them. You know the statement, 'People don't care what you know until they know that you care.' I mention this all the time in coaching my managers on how to coach. It's important that they get started coaching and active with employees. Part of their growth and development is getting started in the process. Employees appreciate positive attention. Coaching is positive attention."

"Super. My next question: Wouldn't you say that most of your managers are promoted from your ranks of employees, therefore they were probably very successful employees?" I asked.

"With that question I give a caution," Mr. Scott replied. "Not every highly successful employee can be a manager. In fact, many fail at management because they lack people skills, open-mindedness and coaching skills. Because of their success, some may have a lack of humility. Arrogant managers, even if successful in an employee position, will fail in leadership if they lack humility. Many times they'll lack patience in the process. Perhaps to them, success came naturally so they can't comprehend what is so difficult. This is why I look for the qualities of good character, good people skills, a patient countenance, an open mind, and the ability to coach. With the ability to coach, they will have the skill of breaking things down to teach the fundamentals.

"I like to point to Tommy Lasorda, Pat Riley, or Phil Jackson as examples of great coaches. Yet as players they were not the best. I believe Tommy Lasorda only pitched three innings in the major leagues. But what each man has is an understanding of the fundamentals and their importance of execution. Each has good character, and as leaders will lead by example and earn respect. It's important how they carry themselves. Each one has strong people skills and a strong ability to coach. Their players would rave on how they break down the fundamentals and teach them. So don't get caught up that your managers had to be star employees. I've had good managers I hired from other industries, other departments, within the current employee ranks yet not superstars, and some that were superstar employees. As each starts coaching and showing that they care, you'll see employees will respond and follow.

"To use a superstar as an example, look at the basketball legend Magic Johnson. Magic had natural skills and talent, was a playing superstar, and worked hard on his game. But in an interview after Magic Johnson gave up coaching, he stated he didn't have the patience for the players. He was naturally talented and had a strong work ethic. Magic had a difficult time understanding others who didn't have the same. Magic had the self-reflection to realize it."

"You make a good point. How does coaching relate to cause and effect?"

"It is everything in relation to cause and effect. We all have heard the statement that insanity is doing the same thing but expecting a different result. If a bad result occurs and you do the same thing again, that's insane. So we look at it from a different perspective. We've witnessed good results and what behaviors drove those results. As we coach, we teach and coach through the process to duplicate those causes because we know they arrive at good results. Duplicating the same good thing is intelligent. Also as coaches, we work with an open mind to fine tune and improve and understand that things are always evolving. We're not afraid of change, or taking a calculated risk, but we stay observant. This is what a coach does."

"Are there certain aspects that concern you when you make a change or adjustment?"

"Certainly. We must always ask why we need change. What cause brought us to what effect? Many times as we define the answers, what we realize is we were not executing the proper cause. We go back to basics to execute. If we determine execution isn't the problem, then we dissect the cause piece by piece. This will determine if we need a little change, or wholesale changes. Other factors to consider are other variables in your business. Has your market changed or evolved in any way? What factors has the economy had on you? What about your demographics? All these can be factors but with whatever change you choose, or if you choose no change, always clarify accountability. In all methods, systems, philosophies, etc., we must ask, 'How do we help keep the employee honest?' This is not honesty such as theft but an honesty of accountability. How will I hold each employee accountable, each manager, and myself? Don't implement anything new or different without defining the answer to this question. It's that accountability that helps everyone grow. But you also must ask, 'How do I measure that accountability?'"

"Is this where rewards or consequences comes into effect?" I asked.

"You encountered rewards or consequence philosophy in every aspect of what we implemented. I am sure that you recognized it meeting with each manager. Rewards or consequence is a driving force with anything you're implementing. Whether it's correcting shortcuts, confronting situations, solving problems, setting goals, etc., all deal with behavior, so rewards or consequences is the key. Understand, I can't always control what people do, but I can control what I reward. This is exactly what coaches do."

"Is this where you created your philosophy on playing favorites?"

"I didn't create it. It is what coaches do. Emmitt Smith, the running back for the Dallas Cowboys was a favorite of coach Jimmy Johnson. It wasn't just because of his skills, but Emmitt was a leader. He worked hard in practice, listened to the coaches, studied film, and always gave 110%. In sports, no one faults a coach for having the right favorites. It should be no different in business as long as it's for the right reasons such as hard work, good effort and behavior, listening to management, and being a team player. Playing favorites is simply standing on the values and principles that you're putting forth which sends that message to every employee. If you play favorites for the wrong reasons, such as to appease an employee, you will breed bad character and send the wrong message."

"What do you mean to appease an employee?"

"Here is what I mean. I've seen managers not stand on their values and principles because they are afraid of losing a certain employee. I've even seen them hire back employees who left, sacrificing their principles. We see the same in professional sports where a player pouts and causes distractions on the team. The good coaches stand on their principles and either the player changes, or the coach eliminates them. The coach understands what message he is sending. The coach also realizes that the decision, in a long term view, is a better move. He may face short term effects, but would be worse off by not standing on his values and principles. A coach truly does this for the team and has no problem expressing it as such."

"Mr. Scott, you certainly are a good coach and manager. Did I tell you it was a former employee who first told me about you? I also talked with other former employees and some of your previous employers. I commend you on the positive feedback and compliments. I am impressed how highly they regard you and this business."

"Thank you, that is humbling. That goes back to my message and belief that how others talk about you is how you're perceived. This perception is important and valuable. For example, I am a Kansas City Chief fan. I remember reading an article many years back, when the Chiefs signed Kendrell Bell, the linebacker who played for the Pittsburg Steelers. When Bell was deciding which team to sign with, he had a conversation with the Chiefs' running back Priest Holmes, who was also a personal friend. Holmes stated that the Chiefs were an honest organization. This is a high compliment said about an employer, and a key quality that Kendrell Bell valued and he subsequently signed with the Chiefs. This works the same in business. If we focus on being an honest organization and put forth the right values and principles, the perception of a good organization comes naturally. The other natural benefit is employees take ownership and accountability. Simply put, if I can get more people to manage my business other than myself, then I have a more effective business."

"How do you begin accomplishing that? How do you make a game plan, and how do you manage its execution?" I asked.

"Well, you have to start somewhere. If you wait for better conditions, you'll never start. This is why I say it is so important to get your managers to start coaching right away. From there you can work on their development along with any needed personnel changes. The columnist Liz Smith once stated, 'Begin somewhere; you cannot build a reputation on what you intend to do.' As a head coach, or a manager of a department, take an inventory of yourself, your staff and employees, and your business. This inventory should define an assessment of where you are, and where you'd like to be. In defining employees, you'll define their qualities and assess their potential for growth.

"A manager or coach defines a game plan. At first, the plan is, 'How can I win with my current players?' Many do not ask themselves this question because they'd rather think of making changes before they start coaching. You must start coaching immediately and work your process as you coach. So the next question would be, 'What type of players do I need to improve and grow?' This is a continual part of your inventory. From there you ask and define, 'How long do I allow, and what are my stages?' By asking this you break down your stages and long term goals into short term goals. This allows you to play the game now and continually work your game plan going forward. Another question is one you'll ask many times. 'When and how do I make adjustments?' This prepares you to realize that adjustments are needed. What are your alternate plans? Finally, another question to be cognizant of is, 'When do I realize I have the wrong game plan?' This question is not a doubting question but an evaluation question. How do you assess your progress? When do you make wholesale changes or stop completely and change directions? Without asking this, you'll fail to post warning signs or signs of caution in your mind. It might be asked at a later time but by then it might be too late. You ignored what would have been the warning signs and you've let failure in that is difficult to reverse."

"I understand your opinion and view point. But why not work your changes first, and then start coaching?" I asked.

"Because it never works that way and you'll never assess whether you have the right coaches or managers to begin with. What if you get your dream team in place and then realize your coaches are wrong? The quicker you start giving the right attention through coaching, your other changes and adjustments are smoother and accepted. Not confronting and coaching is really just an excuse to put coaching off for whatever reasons you create. I'll give you an example. There is a manager, Marvin, in another business I know whose business is starting to suffer. Needless to say, his employees are suffering and lacking growth and development. Marvin is trying to recruit and hire successful employees from our other locations or former employees. I'm not saying this is a bad idea, I believe in adding good proven employees, but Marvin is looking at this solution as his problem solver. His current employees suffer because they have no coaching. This is why his business is suffering. He's looking for a quick solution, but lacks long-term foresight. If he would work and implement coaching through all his managers, his current employees and business will benefit. This will also allow him to take an accurate inventory and assessment of personnel and the business plan. Any new employees and recruits will then be inserted in a much healthier environment."

"I've heard others express similar sentiment as taking a reality check. Is this basically what you are saying?" I asked.

"Part of it is a reality check," Mr. Scott replied. "I call that part the 'Elvis Presley is dead' realization. It's the first thing that we must realize and quit fooling ourselves. From there an honest evaluation will lay the foundation to build upon. There are no magic pills or magic bullets. It starts by this inventory and game plan. Within the game plan are our hiring practices, which are part of the foundation. Everything takes planning and execution. Following up and managing this process are what coaches do."

"In speaking with Mr. Douglas, I did find it interesting that you seem to be in a continual hiring mode." I smiled.

"We always look for good people to add to our team. There are times that we may be doing more ramping up, but we keep a process in place at all times to allow us to continually upgrade when a good hire comes along. If you are not in a continual hiring process, then as needs arise you are more likely to hire in desperation. It's at these times that you'll make bad choices. To always be looking and willing to add talent builds a stronger organization and also keeps current employees honest in their quality of work. If I am coaching a team, I always want to add talent. This is what coaches do."

"Is this why you are involved in the hiring, because of its importance?" I asked.

"Yes! If you don't learn how to hire good quality personnel, you'll never achieve the ultimate success you desire. You are actually more likely to fail. In sports, you see the head coach involved on draft day as well as the ownership."

"I truly see the benefit and message you send by your involvement. You're telling your current employees and managers how important it is to you to bring on good personnel to the team. You're also telling applicants how important the decision is on bringing them on by your involvement. This is one of the many things that impresses me is the message that you send, as well as how you treat your employees. Mr. Douglas's sign that 'Everyone is a 10' is a good philosophy," I said.

"Every person is a ten," Mr. Scott stated. "We treat each person with respect. In return we receive respect. As we treat people right and continually bring good people on board, good things happen. Our business grows, our morale increases, and opportunities open for others to advance. This occurs within our business and throughout our corporation. If someone advances, it increases morale and we assist in their advancement."

"Yes, I've heard that you continually have key personnel advance. I'm impressed that you help and encourage the process. I've witnessed environments where management discouraged and even prevented others from advancing outside their individual business because they did not want to lose employees or start a trend." I said.

"This is short sighted thinking, Mr. Scott replied. "I certainly understand about protecting against customers or competitors hiring your personnel. That is just good business. But employees' advancement in your organization sends a positive message, increases morale and productivity, and opens up more opportunity. Now wouldn't you be more motivated working for an organization where you have witnessed this opportunity? I have even assisted employees advancing with positions with our partners in business. I do have a policy to protect myself on how partners may wish to hire one of our employees, but this has even strengthened our partnership environment. To prevent this opportunity would only send the wrong message and lower morale. I'd probably lose that employee by closing that opportunity. That is not a good result."

"So you believe that a good coach helps players advance?"

"Absolutely, it is what coaches do. I remember reading about the San Antonio Spurs organization.[19] Over a ten-year period, the Spurs have had the highest winning percentage in sports. Yet over this time they have had key personnel hired and promoted outside their organization. Each year they lose their assistant coaches because others want to emulate their success. When asked about their philosophy and the effect of its implementation, the owner, Peter Holt, made this statement. 'You hate to lose people that have helped create the success you have. But at the same time, new people come in and bring new ideas, and new blood.' You see, new personnel keep them fresh and motivated instead of stale. Peter Holt further expressed the Spurs philosophy. 'As long as you respect the organization, the organization will do its best to advance your career."[20] If you know your employer will do their best to advance your career, your effort and productivity will be honest. So yes, this is what winning coaches do."

"I have witnessed other organizations holding people back for fear of losing people. Only now do I realize how that approach is short sighted." I stated.

"That's the point," Mr. Scott said. "A coach is focused on his players' growth and success. A good coach makes it about their players, not about themselves. Grow others around you. Give others the credit for improvements and you'll increase their morale and efforts. With this comes loyalty and success. Successful employees create a successful business. Your efforts will permeate through others and your value is evident. You will not have to point out your involvement or details. It will be known. This is why everything evolves around behavior. Realizing this, you then can break down any area and make a game plan. Rewards or consequence is a tool to correct, modify, and improve behavior."

"So what are the foundations of behavior modification?"

"First we define the goal of behavior change. Behavior change is changing the results by changing the intentions of the individual. Simply put, their behavior is their intentions on what result they want. Some may be misguided or blind to their intentions. A coach must recognize that."

"What's the one key to behavior change?" I asked. "If you could just tell someone to make a change and they do it, that would be simple. But it never is that easy, is it?"

"No, it isn't," Mr. Scott answered. "This is where many get it wrong because they do not understand how our minds work. The one key is to first understand this fact. I took a course called Project Metamorphosis[21] that defines how we each are to a great extent what we believe about ourselves and how we talk to ourselves inside our minds. Most people make three kinds of comments to themselves: child comments, critic comments, and adult comments."

"Can you define each?" I asked.

"Sure, I'll summarize. The child comments come from our early development, but no matter what age we are, we never lose the child voice; it stays with us for life. A child's point of view wants to have fun and have it now. The child doesn't like to do anything boring, dull, or distasteful. The child may be manipulative and tries to do things to avoid work. It is short sighted and doesn't think about the future or goals. The child wants what it wants now no matter what happens later. It prefers to play or watch TV or do anything that keeps them from getting to the business at hand. The child usually thinks in first-person in terms of 'I want/what's in it for me.' Luckily the child in you often responds to logic and rewards. Thus, when you have work to do, you tell your child that a reward will come after, perhaps cookies or a play break. Although you are working toward future goals, you need to give immediate feedback and rewards. The child comments in your mind include: I'm bored, I'm tired, this is no fun, that's too much work, I don't like this, I don't want to do that, what is the point? Nobody else has to do that, why am I treated like this? It's not fair."[22]

"Okay, and so what about critic comments?" I asked.

"Critic comments are often the second type of inner comments that we develop. These comments first came from others and take the form of a second person directed to you. The critic is kind of a watch-dog gone out of control. The critic causes you to doubt your abilities, goals, and self. It says that a task is too hard. It says you have the wrong background or ability to get the job done so why even try? Worry is the critic's chief activity. An example would be spending more time worrying more about finding a job than applying for one. The critic reminds you that you are destined for failure. These comments are less easy to control. An individual will internalize their critics' comments as part of their belief system about themselves. Thus the same logical approach you used to control the child comments often fails. You'll find you can't out-talk the critic. Instead you must replace the critic comments with more appropriate ones. You start by replacing any negative with positives. Instead of, 'You're never going to get a good job,' say 'I have developed some new skills that will help me get a good job.' It takes time to control the critic. We have to remember that we cannot bargain with the critic. Only long-term efforts replacing critic comments with adult comments will change them."

"Wow. I have a critic inside me. What about the adult comments, how do they work?" I asked.

"The adult in you is the voice of reason and logic. It knows that some things are no fun but must be done anyway. It recognizes that you're not perfect, but that you are a person of value. The adult looks for solutions, learns from past mistakes, and supports future efforts. Because the adult is in control of yourself, you think in first person, I. Now problem solving and decision making are the adult's strengths. The adult thinks about what it takes to achieve goals. It acts accordingly. The adult has a plan and follows it. The adult will recognize mistakes and makes changes for the future. The adult voice will say, 'This is difficult but I chose to do it. I wasn't able to succeed before but I now have some new strategies. I'm a different person than I was then. I am thinking differently than I used to. And, I am making different decisions than I used to make.' If you pay attention, you'll find that your voices talk all the time. They talk to you in social and family situations. They talk to you about how you learn. This is how each comment drives us."

"So how does this play into behavior change?" I asked.

"Understanding how these comments work, and what order each has developed, child, critic, then adult, we learn to manage on the positive effect of each. The foundation of behavior is developed first from those child comments. The child will listen to logic, but only with rewards or consequences. Rewards or consequences play to the very foundation of change to get that child to accept logic which allows the child to correct themselves toward the right behavior. If we have laid this foundation, then next we make sure we cover the critic comments. First, we don't belittle anyone, period. To belittle someone would only bring out the critic comments. No matter what, we are respectful. This is why we show human value. After all, everyone is a ten, whether successful with us or not. We correct constructively. This is where factual not negative is powerful. Factual not negative avoids bringing out the critic in individuals. You see, only with covering the child comments in individuals and the critic comments can we ever get to the adult comments. The adult comments are the stage of development and results. At this stage we can grow the individual to new heights.

"However it is imperative to always manage effectively to the child and the critic comments in each individual, or else you regress. Now it's the adult in us that allows us to respond to 'trust yet verified,' or 'shortcuts get you lost.' With these, the child wants to accept and make the change but the adult does the actual changing. This is why behavior change is similar in children and adults, because that child comment development is our foundation. Good coaches realize this and manage through this perspective. After all, isn't that what coaches do?"

"So we should always be correcting?" I asked.

"If correction is needed then the answer is yes," Mr. Scott replied. "Behavioral change is continual, not just a zap it once and it's done. I've learned if I am not correcting then I am enabling. If my daughter doesn't keep her room clean, and I do not correct her, then I am enabling her to break my rules. More than that, I'm telling her it is okay."

"What about letting employees know you're angry?" I questioned.

Mr. Scott replied. "First, being factual is imperative, because the facts don't change. I've learned that to ignore the facts doesn't change the facts. The facts hide nothing. Second, there is a difference in anger and disappointment. Anger will play to those negative critic comments and the individual will regress or slow in development. But I do let someone know that I am disappointed. That's a factual statement. Sometimes I may be disappointed because I expected better. I simply express it in those terms. This method plays to the logic in the child other than the criticism of the critic."

"I see. It all makes sense. So it's the child comments that will talk to us first?" I asked.

"Yes, because we developed them first. Earlier we talked about how all things must be reciprocal. If we say, trust yet verified, yet do not practice it, then it's the child in an individual that will point it out. The child comments will say, 'It's not fair!' etc. This is what holds us accountable. That child looks for accountability."

"That makes sense to me. Mr. Scott, you mentioned shortcuts. How important is it to correct shortcuts early on?" I was deeply enjoying our conversation.

"Very important. The longer you let it go then the individuals perception is that the shortcut is okay. By not correcting it, you'll add to the child comments logic, and the critic comments justification. Once it hits the adult stage, it has grown to the perception that it must be okay. Let me use a story I read in a Kenneth Copeland magazine[23] where Kenneth describes going to his first baseball game. Everything happened pretty much as he expected. When a batter connected with a pitch, he headed straight for first base. He certainly did not take off running toward the pitcher's mound and then on to second base. If he had, they would have laughed him off the field. People would have shaken their heads and said, 'That fool has lost his mind! That's a big league player, too. Whatever happened to first base?'"

Mr. Scott continued, "Of course, it sounds silly to even suggest a professional ball player would skip first base. He would get no positive results for himself or for his team. He could run hard. He could run with a lot of style. But he'd get called out just the same. The rules are the same, whether it's the major leagues or a local high school team. Kenneth Copeland also states, 'We can't skip first base and expect to get results, though many people try!'"

Mr. Scott sighed and continued, "The shortcut in a baseball game sounds absurd because it is so blatant. But the difference in our work environments is we help mask and cover up shortcuts instead of standing on the rules of the game. When we don't expose shortcuts then they don't look absurd and will even look normal. Exposing shortcuts and correcting them as early as possible is what coaches do."

"That's a great example. But in business doesn't it get harder to identify? How do you recognize a shortcut?" I asked.

"This is why I have active managers. We coach. Coaching is being active daily with our employees and involved with them always. Experience tells us the most effective way. We teach our coaches the most effective way so they will recognize any variance. In the banking industry, when they teach about identifying counterfeit money they use real money. They don't get their employees involved or exposed to counterfeit at all. They have their employees study the real thing. By knowing the real thing, they can identify what isn't."

"Thanks, another great example. Now what about when you can't change someone's perception or it is too difficult?"

"In a book Mrs. Kendall shared with me,[24] the authors talk about how prejudices can taint our observations and objectivity. They tell about a teen boy named Johnny who wakes up one day to go to the beach."

"Yes, Mrs. Kendall shared that story with me about how the boy kept seeing signs and messages but refused to accept them for what they were." I said.

"Exactly, the book goes on to discuss more of Johnny's blindness but what you get out of it is an individual who truly wants to be blind to the truth. These individuals will lie to themselves and never get past the child comment stage. They will not grow or change. Think of the classic story of the Three Little Pigs. There is another version called, 'The True Story of the Three Little Pigs, written by A. Wolf' where the wolf gives his side of the story. He tells how he simply needed to borrow a cup of sugar and so he went to ask the pigs. He had a cold and when he sneezed, he blew their houses down. The pigs died accidentally so how could he waste a free meal? Here is someone that rationalizes and fights the truth. They cannot get past the critic comment stage and will not develop. Attempts will be futile and a waste of energy. Worst yet, that attitude can spread to others. You need to identify these types and eliminate them. These types are cancers and cancer needs to be cut out."

"You mentioned cancers; can you expand on cancers in a business?" I asked.

"Well, the first thing a coach does is to try not to add one to the team. Much can be defined through the hiring process. Even if the person had prior success, but if they have an attitude that nothing was their fault, that should raise an alarm. Checking past employers and references will give indicators. If you hear that the person could do well if he has changed, or if you can control certain elements, then you need to pass on that person."

"So no matter how successful they may have been elsewhere, if you determine they are a cancer, you pass on hiring them?" I asked.

"Yes. You cannot train character. A cancer is a person with bad character. We cannot take someone with bad character and train them to good character. Character is something that is developed over time, starting with childhood. When I say character, I mean good character with the right values and principles, which create automatic responses. A person either has good character or bad character. It's established."

"Mr. Charles spoke on this. He stated that only something drastic or divine changes character." I commented.

"I agree," Mr. Scott said. "I've seen people of bad character lose a loved one suddenly and the loss changes their value system, therefore it changes their principles. Other times people will finally get tired of their character traits and reach for that something divine. Unfortunately, we are neither drastic nor divine. When we recognize someone with bad character, we eliminate them. A coach must recognize this as quickly as possible and define it as such. A coach will not waste any more time or energy trying to change that person. The longer the cancer stays, the more it spreads and infects others."

"Why are people cancerous?"

"That's a good question. Many do not realize they are cancers. They are blind to the truth. A cancerous person is quick to point the finger but not to take responsibility. Some people are just discontent, bitter, or jealous and we don't always know why. In the Bible, there are characters like Absalom who rose up against his father King David. I believe people that have bad character have what I call the spirit of Absalom. Absalom wasn't satisfied. But because King David brought Absalom back and let his cancer mature and grow, it spread. Then you had those that followed Absalom, because he infected them. A cancer will eventually reveal itself."

Mr. Scott grabbed a dictionary and read, "Cancer; 'A pernicious spreading of evil; example, a cancer of bigotry spread through the community.' Pernicious means causing great harm; destructive; ruinous. If you have a person who will cause great harm, why keep them?

Remember, if a positive attitude is contagious, why wouldn't a cancerous one be also?"

"Mr. Charles said pretty much the same thing. What are the indicators that show you have people of good character?" I asked.

"Good character is doing the right thing when nobody is looking. If this is what you have in employees, then your job is easier. But a coach will still coach along with checks and balances. A coach will understand his player's individual perspectives. Understanding how others view things defines a person."

"How is that?" I asked.

"I read a book called *The Spirit of Faith*[25] by Mark Hankins. Mr. Hankins states that a person cannot be negative, critical, and constantly complaining and claim to have a spirit of faith.[26] He tells a story about a man who was asleep in his bedroom, and some friends played a joke on him. While he was sleeping, they wiped a piece of limburger cheese under his nose. Immediately the man woke up and exclaimed, 'Man, it sure stinks in here!' He walked out of his bedroom and into the living room and said, 'It stinks in here!' Then he walked into the kitchen and said, 'It stinks in here!' He went out the front door, looked at the sky, breathed in deeply, and said, 'The whole world stinks!' The lesson is that anytime it stinks everywhere you go, the stink is underneath your nose. You are carrying the stink with you."[27]

"What about coaches that are cancers? Mr. Charles talked about this." I said.

"First I wouldn't call them coaches, but they may be in management. I have seen many cancerous people in authority. It really is a shame. Some very intelligent and talented people have a cancerous character, yet gain authority. This is why in the hiring process good character must be the first thing an employee has. An individual with no good character traits equates to no job no matter how much talent.

If I had a potential hire with all the talent and skills but had bad character, I would not hire them. If I had another candidate with good character, with some talent and skill, yet were trainable, I would hire that candidate instead. A coach must make good character their priority. Fortunately, we come across many with good character and talent. But always remember the formula, hire character, train skills."

"I agree, but what about that person in authority that has bad character?" I asked.

"Well," Mr. Scott replied, "first understand that a person that is in authority that has a cancerous character has a reprobate mind which expects certain things and they are typically ungrateful. A thankful person is a coach and this person wishes and seeks to give thanks. Which one would you want to work for?"

"The coach obviously."

"Yes, but the cancerous person in authority has a foothold. With this foothold they eliminate coaching opportunities due to their character. Employees become reluctant to bring issues to this person. We describe it as walking on eggshells. Also some cancers in authority distance themselves from areas of need, so they'll be less accountable. A coach seeks those areas of need and assumes responsibility."

"So how do they obtain this position of authority?" I asked.

"High intelligence and talents. Employers desire that intelligence and talent so they may be blind to the cancerous character. Others will blind themselves to the cancerous character believing the intelligence, talents and skills outweigh the cancerous character. This is a major mistake. The employer believes they can manage around the character or change it. What eventually happens is that the employer is walking on eggshells and that cancer will spread.

"A talented person who is a cancer has a false sense of worth in regards to their employer because of their skills, talents, or intellect.

The scary aspect is they also can convince others of this worth. A cancerous person will often believe they are owed more because of their talents, but isn't that why their employer is employing them?"

"Yes, it is," I said. "We all are hired because the employer expects us to show our skills and talent for their benefit. For this we are paid."

"Exactly, but a cancerous person in authority is a danger," Mr. Scott stated. "One, they will infect their employees. Two, they'll establish a stronghold as they infect because of the false perception that their talent and skills are more valuable. Three, they'll stranglehold their superiors to keeping them, either because of fear of losing employees or convincing themselves they are managing this person. Both are a falsehood.

"We once had a vice president at one of our locations who needed to make a change in top management. The location wasn't performing well and the manager, Timothy, was a cancer. Timothy was left in place so long he had a stronghold over the employees. Because he was talented, he convinced the employees that the problems weren't because of him, so the employees believed that the corporate office and their direction was the problem. Our vice president, Jeremy, had just taken over the territory. He recognized and defined the cancer right away. Jeremy immediately defined a game plan and recruited a replacement that Jeremy knew would coach. Timothy knew things weren't going well, and he voiced his complaints to his employees as a cancer would do. One of the top employees met with Jeremy and stated point blank that if Jeremy fired Timothy, he would walk."

"What happened?" I asked.

Mr. Scott continued, "Jeremy knew he still had to make a change. He believed that even if he lost a few employees the long term benefit would be better. So he let Timothy go, quietly and professionally. Then, before announcing and introducing the new manager, Jeremy pulled that one employee into a private meeting. Jeremy told him that he valued him and respected him as an employee. He informed him that he did make a management change, as ultimately it was his responsibility for improving the location. Jeremy stated he felt it was important to privately notify this employee out of respect and because of their prior meeting. He explained he believed the new manager would make an immediate impact and asked the employee to stay on board and give him the benefit of the doubt."

"And how did the employee respond?" I asked.

"The employee was disappointed that Timothy was let go but appreciative on how Jeremy handled it. He agreed to stay on."

"So what was the final outcome?"

"The new manager did have an immediate impact. The employee who had threatened to quit loved the new manager, as did all the employees. When a true coach arrives, others see it and rally around it. The location grew and people developed. But look at what Jeremy did when he encountered this circumstance."

"What's that?" I asked.

"He coached. He determined the right values and principles and stuck to them. He confronted the issue, instead of avoiding it. Avoiding it might have lost him an employee. Jeremy showed integrity and respect, because everyone is a ten. He was factual, not negative. He showed humility, not puffing up at the employee's threat. After all, isn't this what coaches do? He knew the employees were led astray. Many managers will rise up in arrogance when someone threatens to quit. Jeremy recognized it for what it was."

I appreciated Mr. Scott's examples. "Mr. Charles talked about employees hiring back cancerous managers or employees. Why do they do that?"

"For many reasons," Mr. Scott said. "The employer may believe they can change the individual. They may have many talents, skills, and intellect that the employer desires and they fool themselves that the person has changed, or that they can manage around the cancer, or that the person's talents, skills, and intellect outweigh the cancer. It's always it's a mistake."

"Can you give me an example?"

"Sure. I had a friend, Bobby, who was an assistant manager at a pizza parlor. Bobby noticed that a delivery employee, Eddie, was creating duplicate orders to claim free pizza that he would eat or give away to his friends. Bobby fired Eddie, but eventually hired him back. They then caught Eddie stealing from the cash register. Eddie's character had not changed. We need to make decisions based on values and principles, and we cannot accept bad character no matter how talented an employee may be or if we feel sorry for him or if we even like him. People need to remember the story about the frog and the scorpion."

"The frog and the scorpion?" I asked.

"The frog and the scorpion were on one side of a pond with both needing to get to the other side. The frog makes a deal with the scorpion and tells him, 'I'll let you ride on my back, if you promise not to sting me.' They agreed and started across. About halfway across the pond, the scorpion could not help himself and stings the frog. The frog cries out, 'Why did you do that? Now we'll both die!' The scorpion answered, 'What did you expect? I'm a scorpion.' So they both drowned. No matter what, the scorpion couldn't change his nature. If you hire a person for an authoritative role who you know has bad character, don't be surprised when they sting you."

"I've heard the story before, and it really fits here. I guess it's hard sometimes if your business is struggling, or you really wish to improve it," I said.

"I've seen people rehire managers with bad character and they believe they set the groundwork to avoid the pitfalls of that cancer.

They'll discuss it directly with that person, warning them that certain past behaviors aren't allowed. Always it's a mistake. Like the scorpion, it's in their nature. That nature will eventually show itself."

"How do you recognize cancers in authority?" I asked.

"A cancer is the same whether in authority or an employee. They're complainers, nothing is their fault. They believe they have the answers, yet avoid responsibility. They have an inflated perception of themselves and wish to show it. They tend to have big egos, and they show it. I remember one manager who was a cancer who lined his bookshelf so everyone could visibly see all the management learning skills books he's read. This was more about ego than about the material in the books. In truth, I'd rather see him implement what he's read and I wouldn't need to see the books, nor would the employees. Many managers that are cancers want others to know how much knowledge they have, but they all lack the key element for true success."

"What's that, Mr. Scott?"

"People skills. They all lack people skills. Sure, some may have some success and fool their employers. They may even develop a fan club which they'll point to. But the truth is they are a cancer and need to be cut out. The point that they fooled their employer or have a fan club is only because they've been allowed to grow and infest. A coach must recognize cancers and eliminate them as soon as possible. After all, that's what coaches do."

"So, it's as simple as that, cut it out?" I queried.

"Absolutely! Look, sometimes we must make difficult decisions. I knew a general manager, Marcus, of another business who had a top manager, Leslie, that was a cancer. Leslie had worked there for some time, very intelligent, talented, and well versed in the business. Marcus hired a second manager, Chris, within the same role as Leslie. Marcus did this in an attempt to expand and grow. Chris was a coach, and his people responded to him. He also confronted issues, and brought about the need to make improvements and changes. At first, Marcus, the GM, spoke of how he liked Chris because Chris made him confront issues and positive changes started to occur. But Leslie, the cancer, wasn't changing, so it became a battle to reinforce the positive. Masking or medicating the situation can only have temporary effects. Chris had an impact on his direct reports but could not affect the whole business or the other employees not reporting to him. Internal struggles like this happen all the time."

"So what happened in this circumstance?"

"There was some improvement but not wholesale improvement. Marcus who had enjoyed the fact that Chris brought forward issues to confront soon grew tired of that very same aspect. You see, unless he was going to take action then it became a burden to look at issues. Marcus would not admit it, but he became satisfied with the status quo. With no commitment to confront issues, the business stayed in a staggered state. Soon Marcus needed to make financial cutbacks. When assessing who he would release, he made the simple decision based on seniority. So Chris was let go and Leslie stayed on. Marcus believed he owed it to Leslie because Leslie had been with him so long."

"I see. Marcus simply did not want to confront the situation," I said.

"You're learning. Good job! Now you see why confrontation is a benefit. We must confront situations to correct them and get through them. With confrontation we'll learn and grow. I remember another general manager, Clifford, talking with other GMs about a manager on his staff. Clifford spoke of how the manager, Sam, just didn't seem happy. Clifford believed this affected Sam's performance as well as the employees around Sam. When asked by one of the other general managers what he had done to rectify the situation, Clifford stated nothing. By doing nothing, Clifford allowed the situation to grow and affect other employees. Confrontation must be daily as things occur. A football coach will not wait until after the game to tell a player he's not blocking correctly. He'll confront it quickly to correct it and move past it. Like I said before, isn't that what coaches do?"

"Yes," I agreed. "Mr. Charles mentioned about sharing yourself with employees and that it is instrumental in team building."

"Yes. This is why I admire Dick Vermeil, former coach of the Kansas City Chiefs. He's personable to his players. When I take a location, I take extra time and effort to share myself. After work, before work, and at lunch time, etc., I stay and talk about regular stuff, about my family and about my dreams. When I'd take the time to share, employees share the same with me. I'm not different than they are because I hold a position of authority. It actually brings them to respect that authority. But because I'm real, I can ask them for extra effort, or tell them when I'm disappointed. It builds a better environment."

"I may be jumping around in my notes, but this sounds like what Mrs. Kendall spoke of, looking at the man in the mirror, and putting your people's success first." I stated.

"Yes, you're correct," Mr. Scott said. "If we ask others to look at themselves honestly, then we must also do the same. We must show it first. If we demonstrate that we're real and not phony, then so will the employees. Putting your people's success first is what a true coach does. Successful people surround themselves with successful people. It's only smart to create that success in others. That's what coaches do."

"Yes, and setting high expectations," I said.

"Yes. That's a function of a coach. Imagine a running back telling his coach, 'Coach, I think I'll gain a total of forty yards today.' Well, that coach will or should immediately set higher expectations. These expectations will be based on the player's skill level, on need, and also on outside factors such as the offensive line. Now the coach isn't just going to say, 'Oh no, you'll gain 100 yards today,' and walk away. No, he'll probably first find out why the player only believes he'll gain forty. He'll then break down to the player how he should and can gain more. He'll make the player practice and follow his blocks. But all the way through this process, the coach will coach the player. Business is the same way."

"Is there anything else you must show your employees or players?" I asked.

"Yes, you must give them a vision. Vision is the key for higher expectations. I once read an article in *The Guidepost* magazine[28] about a karate instructor named Rav G. His students were children with cancer. Rav G. taught karate to help these young cancer patients overcome fears, and then overcome cancer. He teaches that in karate, before you break a board you must imagine yourself breaking it first. So before they can beat cancer, they must imagine beating it first. He teaches them to imagine first and conquer second. This is a key to his students' success. So a coach teaches players to envision their success first, and then conquer it. A coach is responsible for their players' focus. This must be done on individual goals, even if results are taking time. After all, this is what coaches do."

"So a coach doesn't warn them of the pitfalls or dangers?" I asked.

"Sure they do. But they don't focus them on it. What you do and what you think makes all the difference. Visualize yourself on where you want to be."

"Yes, I talked about this with Mr. Anthony," I said. "I enjoyed how he designed his focus as a baseball game. Having home plate as values and principles showed me the importance on how this is where everything begins."

"You're correct," Mr. Scott said. "A bank robber isn't void of values and principles. He simply has the wrong ones. When someone keeps getting bad results, we must identify their values and principles and correct them. On a football team, a player may be lazy and not practice. The player may believe they are above practicing or that they know better. The coach must identify this and correct the players' values and principles. This is why we ourselves must manage with correct values and principles. It starts with us. Identifying values and principles is what coaches do."

"Good point. Mr. Anthony also talked about not making decisions in anger."

"Yes, it is very dangerous," Mr. Scott replied. "In fact, that cancerous person in authority tends to make decisions out of anger. We know we don't want to be like that. Now the key is to not get angry, then you'll not make decisions in anger."

"Not get angry? Is that possible?" I asked.

"There is a difference in being angry and being disappointed. It does take practice. But everything we implement is designed around that. This is why we have factual not negative. When we keep it factual, you manage away from that anger. When you show everyone is a ten, you believe in their value as a person. So if something flares you up, you know to step away. The more you work on it, the more you'll grow."

"That sounds reasonable. Anyway, how do coaches take problems and make them opportunities?" I asked.

"How a coach reacts to problems is key. A coach has already built an environment to assist in this. Because a coach continually recruits and adds good players, he's more prepared if a player gets hurt. So it's an opportunity for him to play another player and to develop them. It's important to take this perspective when looking at problems. Ask yourself, what opportunity do I have here? After all, this is what coaches do, right?"

"Yes, it is. Mr. Anthony had as third base, knowledge and change. Would you like to expand on how a coach uses knowledge for change?" I asked.

Mr. Scott replied, "A coach gives knowledge on why a change is needed. He'll explain it in simple and factual terms. Then that coach will use knowledge to show what is needed and how to use the new knowledge. The coach must be a part of each process of the change by reinforcing it. A coach has to understand and take the player through it. The player must receive appropriate instructions. The coach just doesn't request a change, give information for the new change, and then leave. The coach stays and participates. This is called practice or role play. With it the coach gives more knowledge. The knowledge serves to increase the players' self-image. Now this isn't inflating their ego but it is giving them a vision of the goal and accomplishment, and even managing by rewards. With each step above and continual support and practice, the player's new skill will grow. The coach doesn't leave the player. The coach works with the player until the vision of the goal comes to fruition. With this comes respect and gratitude. This is what builds rapport and trust. The player and coach want success and improvement and their desire comes from this process. But you can see that the very foundation of this change is knowledge. That's why knowledge is the vehicle for change."

"Thank you, Mr. Scott. I could stay all day asking you questions, but what are some important keys that you would like to leave me with?"

"I guess the first thing is to be more concerned about your character than your reputation. I say that because most people worry about their reputation and do not think about their character. Remember, that a cancerous person in authority thinks about their reputation, but ignores their character. Now I understand that your reputation may open doors, but your character will keep you there. Remember, your character is who you are."

"So if I think more about my character I'll be better long term?" I asked.

"Absolutely, and you'll also be prepared for life's difficulties. Remember, when faced with a crisis, the man of character falls back on himself. A man without character will do what he always does, blame others and accept no responsibility. This is where you see people believing they are the victims. They fall back on their bad character.

"Character is always a first when it comes to hiring. From there I determine if they are trainable. Lastly, would be their talent and skills. If they have bad character, or are not trainable, why would I even care about their talent and skills?"

"Wouldn't you desire someone bent on perfection? Someone focused on getting it right?" I asked.

"A perfectionist is someone I stay away from," Mr. Scott replied. "Julia Cameron, in her book, *The Artist's Way*,[29] said, 'A perfectionist is not a quest for the best. It is a pursuit of the worst in us, the part that tells us nothing we do will ever be good enough, that we should try again.' I desire confident people who aren't afraid of mistakes. When someone says they are a perfectionist, it scares me."

"I like that insight. So what is more important, how we manage people, or the systems we have in place?" I asked.

"Both have importance. With no systems in place, some individual's natural talents and skills will have some success. But with no coaching, or how we manage people, we would lack development, growth, and direction. They each benefit each other, but absolutely the way we manage people is the most important."

"Thank you, I would agree. But it takes a lot of patience," I said.

"Yes, it does," Mr. Scott answered. "Just because I am patient does not mean employees are not held accountable. There is a balance. With patience, you develop people with encouragement and guidance. You hold them to expectations and time frames. Patience is the temperament in which you hold yourself.

"My patience has taught me that sometimes the unconventional works. We all may believe reasons why something will work such as a system in place, but then find it is too difficult to execute. Many times we must be aware of when the remedy is worse than the problem. This is where businesses make wholesale changes, but then can't execute. I'm not afraid of trying things because I'm not afraid of failing. I have more failures than success. But that is why I have success.

"We've all heard the story of a highly successful man being asked the key to his success. He responded, 'good decisions.' When asked how he learned to make good decisions, he responded, 'from experience!' When asked how he gained experience, he responded, 'through knowledge!' When asked how he obtained knowledge, he answered 'bad decisions.' So you see, knowledge is obtained from our learning and some of that learning is failure. It's what we do with that failure that matters. But most important it is not being afraid to fail. Patience has taught me this and much more."

I nodded. "Thank you so much. Before I leave, do you have any final pearls of wisdom?"

Mr. Scott stated, "Again I refer to Mark Hankin's book, *The Spirit of Faith*.[30] He is speaking of the Christian faith, but I correlate it to business. In business, you have Pioneers, Settlers, and Museum Keepers. Pioneers are constantly pressing into new territories. They are the innovators needed in business. Pioneers think of new ideas and explore new territories. Some may be reckless. In the Old West days, the reckless pioneers would go exploring without equipment or supplies. Now the smart pioneers take the right supplies. These pioneers have a plan and a way to get back to safety. A smart pioneer isn't afraid of failure; they just chalk it up to experience. But it is the pioneers that create new territories for their companies.

"The next group is the settlers. The settlers are content to stay in their comfort zone. However, the settlers are useful to the pioneers as they will follow and assist the pioneer on their exploring. The settler will help build new roads along with anything else needed for the exploration and setting up of new territories. However, once the pioneer leaves, the settler will not explore. The settler will stay satisfied with the status quo. It is not that they are afraid of exploring; they're just not cognizant of it.

"The museum keepers are content to dust off the memories of the past. The museum keeper wants to talk about past accomplishments and live off that. They have no desire to explore new territory or even maintain the status quo. The museum keeper lacks desire, period.

"Every business needs pioneers. When a business loses their pioneers, they lose their innovation. When a business loses their innovation, their business becomes stagnant. Eventually competitors will catch the business along with the changes in the industry and economy. Without a pioneer, a settler will and may maintain the status quo for some time, but will have no growth or development. But over time, the business will slide for lack of innovation. Now museum keepers, I have no use for them. In fact, I would classify them as your cancerous individuals pointing back to past glories believing they are owed something. They are not."

"I like this analogy," I said.

Mr. Scott went on. "Good, successful companies reinvent themselves because of their pioneers. Apple Computer continually reinvents themselves with new iPhones, iPads and iMacs, and other new innovations like the Apple Watch. Motorola came out with their Razor phone years ago in which they were told it would be too expensive and now would be considered outdated. They evolved with the droid cellphones and their next advanced models. In their industries, they must evolve quickly or die. We also learn that sometimes the unconventional works and these companies weren't afraid of failure. So in my business I need some pioneers. Now these pioneers can be some managers, but also in employee ranks as it instills enthusiasm. I complement the pioneers with many settlers. I need settlers to clear roads and help through the exploration. It is my responsibility to keep the settlers busy. We do that with the pioneers' innovation. Once again, I have no room for museum keepers. That's it, young man. That's what I leave you with."

"Mr. Scott, I truly wish to thank you. I am impressed by your operation and by your openness and cooperation. I am so impressed that I would like to leave you with my resume. I trust you'll find I have good character and a pioneer spirit. After all, that's why I'm here."

NOTES

1. Brandt, Henry R., and Kerry L. Skinner. *Heart of the Problem.* Nashville, TN: Broadman & Holman, 1997. Print.

2. Ibid.

3. Ibid.

4. Ibid.

5. *The American Heritage Dictionary. Second College Edition.* Boston, MA: Houghton Mifflin, 1991. Print.

6. Ibid.

7. Brandt, Henry R., and Kerry L. Skinner. *Heart of the Problem.* Nashville, TN: Broadman & Holman, 1997. Print.

8. *The American Heritage Dictionary. Second College Edition.* Boston, MA: Houghton Mifflin, 1991. Print.

9. Ibid.

10. Ibid.

11. Brandt, Henry R., and Kerry L. Skinner. *Heart of the Problem*. Nashville, TN: Broadman & Holman, 1997. Print.

12. *The American Heritage Dictionary. Second College Edition*. Boston, MA: Houghton Mifflin, 1991. Print.

13. Ibid.

14. *Have You Checked Your Reflection*, poem written by author.

15. *Employees Mimic What They See*, poem written by author.

16. Geisler, Norman L., and Frank Turek. *I Don't Have Enough Faith to Be an Atheist*. Wheaton, IL: Crossway, 2004. Print.

17. *Coaches*, written by author.

18. Frazee, Bonnie. *Chief Learning Officer Magazine* (2004): n. pag. Print.

19. *San Antonio Express News* 4 June 2005: n. pag. Print.

20. Ibid.

21. Atkinson, Rhonda, Frank Cook, and Carol Goux. *Project Metamorphosis*. Windham School District, n.d. Web.

22. Ibid.

23. Geisler, Norman L., and Frank Turek. *I Don't Have Enough Faith to Be an Atheist*. Wheaton, IL: Crossway, 2004. Print.

24. Scieszka, Jon, and Lane Smith. *The True Story of the Pigs*. New York: Viking Kestrel, 1989. Print.

25. Hankins, Mark. *The Spirit of Faith: Turning Defeat into Victory and Dreams into Reality*. N.p.: Mark Hankins, 2007. Print.

26. Ibid.

27. Ibid.

28. "The Guidepost." *Guideposts* n.d.: n. pag. Web.

29. Cameron, Julia. *The Artist's Way: A Spiritual Path to Higher Creativity*. New York: J.P. Tarcher/Putnam, 2002. Print.

30. Hankins, Mark. *The Spirit of Faith: Turning Defeat into Victory and Dreams into Reality*. N.p.: Mark Hankins, 2007. Print.

www.ingramcontent.com/pod-product-compliance
Lightning Source LLC
Chambersburg PA
CBHW070715220326
41598CB00024BA/3166